The True C

How to Becon

William Fisher Markwick

William Alexander Smith

Alpha Editions

This edition published in 2024

ISBN : 9789362098511

Design and Setting By
Alpha Editions
www.alphaedis.com
Email - info@alphaedis.com

Contents

PREFACE.

This book, intended as a supplementary reader for pupils in the seventh and eighth grades of school, has been prepared with a view to meeting a real need of the times. While there are a large number of text-books, and several readers, dealing with citizenship from the political point of view, the higher aspects of citizenship—the moral and ethical—have been seriously overlooked.

The authors of this work have searched in vain for something which would serve as an aid to the joint development of the natural faculties and the moral instincts, so as to produce a well-rounded manhood, upon which a higher type of citizenship might be built. The development of character appears, to us, to be of far greater importance, in the preparation of the youth for the discharge of the duties of public life, than is mere political instruction; for only by introducing loftier ethical standards can the grade and quality of our citizenship be raised.

It is universally conceded that ethics and civics should go hand in hand; and yet pupils pass through our schools by the thousand, without having their attention definitely called to this important subject; and only an honest desire to aid in improving this state of affairs, has led to the preparation of these pages.

The plan of the book is simple in the extreme. It consists of thirty-nine chapters,—one for each week of the school year;—to eachof which has been prefixed five memory gems; one for each school day. Especial care has been taken to use only such language as will be perfectly intelligible to the pupils for whom it is intended.

The largest possible use has been made of anecdote and incident, so as to quicken the interest and hold the attention to the end. These anecdotes have been selected from every available quarter, and no claim of originality is made concerning them or their use.

Into each of those chapters which have to do directly with the development of the natural faculties, or the moral powers, a "special illustration" has been introduced; this being clearly marked off by the insertion of its title in bold-faced type. To these special illustrations a brief bibliography has been added, in order that a fuller study of the character presented may be readily pursued where deemed desirable. It is hoped that these special illustrations will not only serve to increase the general interest; but that, by thus bringing the pupil into direct contact with these greater minds, ambitions and aspirations may be aroused which shall prove helpful in the later life.

A careful presentation of each separate theme by the teacher, will not only increase the interest in the work of the schoolroom; but, by developing a higher type of citizenship, will be a real service to our nation.

THE AUTHORS.

I.

EDUCATION OF THE NATURAL FACULTIES.

MEMORY GEMS.

Every man stamps his value on himself.—Schiller

No capital earns such interest as personal culture.—President Eliot

The end and aim of all education is the development of character.
—Francis W. Parker

One of the best effects of thorough intellectual training is a
knowledge of our own capacities.—Alexander Bain

Education is a growth toward intellectual and moral perfection.
—Nicholas Murray Butler

Education begins in the home, is continued through the public school and college, and finds inviting and ever-widening opportunities and possibilities throughout the entire course of life. The mere acquisition of knowledge, or the simple development of the intellect alone, may be of little value. Many who have received such imperfect or one-sided education, have proved to be but ciphers in the world; while, again, intellectual giants have sometimes been found to be but intellectual demons. Indeed, some of the worst characters in history have been men of scholarly ability and of rare academic attainments.

The true education embraces the symmetrical development of mind, body and heart. An old and wise writer has said, "Cultivate the physical exclusively, and you have an athlete or a savage; the moral only, and you have an enthusiast or a maniac; the intellectual only, and you have a diseased oddity,—it may be a monster. It is only by wisely training all of them together that the complete man may be found."

To cultivate anything—be it a plant, an animal, or a mind—is to make it grow. Nothing admits of culture but that which has a principle of life capable of being expanded. He, therefore, who does what he can to unfold all his powers and capacities, especially his nobler ones, so as to become a well-proportioned, vigorous, excellent, happy being, practices self-culture, and secures a true education.

It is a commonplace remark that "a man's faculties are strengthened by use, and weakened by disuse." To change the form of statement, they grow when they are fed and nourished, and decay when they are not fed and nourished. Moreover, every faculty demands appropriate food. What nourishes one will not always nourish another. Accordingly, one part of man's nature may grow while another withers; and one part may be fed and strengthened at the expense of another.

In Hawthorne's beautiful allegory, the "Great Stone Face," you remember how the man Ernest, by daily and admiring contemplation of the face, its dignity, its serenity, its benevolence, came, all unconsciously to himself, to possess the same qualities, and to be transformed by them, until at last he stood revealed to his neighbors as the long promised one, who should be like the Great Stone Face. So in every human life, the unrealized self is the unseen but all-powerful force that brings into subjection the will, guides the conduct, and determines the character.

"The early life of Washington is singularly transparent as to the creation and influence of the ideal. We see how one quality after another was added, until the character became complete. Manly strength, athletic power and skill, appear first; then, courtesy and refined manners; then, careful and exact business habits; then, military qualities; then, devotion to public service."

Steadily, but rapidly, the transforming work went on, until the man was complete; the ideal was realized. Henceforth, the character, the man, appears under all the forms of occupation and office. Legislator, commander, president; the man is in them all, though he is none of them.

Half the blunders of humanity come from not knowing one's self. If we overrate our abilities, we attempt more than we can accomplish; if we underrate our abilities we fail to accomplish much that we attempt. In both cases the life loses just so much from its sum of power.

He who might wield the golden scepter of the pen, never gets beyond the plow; or perhaps he who ought to be a shoemaker attempts the artistic career of an Apelles. When a life-work presents itself we ought to be able from our self-knowledge to say, "I am, or am not, fitted to be useful in that sphere."

Sydney Smith represents the various parts in life by holes of different shapes upon a table—some circular, some triangular, some square, some oblong—and the persons acting these parts, by bits of wood of similar shapes, and he says, "we generally find that the triangular person has gotten into the square hole, the oblong into the triangular, and a square fellow has squeezed into the round hole."

A fundamental need is to find out the elements of power within us, and how they can be trained to good service and yoked to the chariot of influence. We need to know exactly for what work or sphere we are best fitted, so that when opportunities for service open before us, we may invest our mental capital with success and profit.

Self-knowledge must not be confused with self-conceit; for it implies no immodesty or egotism. Even if the faithful study of one's self reveals a high order of natural gifts, it is not needful to imitate the son of the Emerald Isle who always lifted his hat and made an obsequious bow when he spoke of himself or mentioned his own name. George Eliot hits off pompous self-conceit happily when she likens its possessor to "a cock that thinks the sun rises in the morning to hear him crow."

Margaret Fuller wrote: "I now know all the people in America worth knowing, and I have found no intellect comparable with my own." Even if she did not overrate herself, such self-estimate implied no little boldness in expression. We also read in Greek history, how, when the commanders of the allied fleets gave in, by request, a list of the names of those who had shown the highest valor and skill at the battle of Salamis, each put his own name first, graciously according to Themistocles, the real hero of the day, the second rank.

Not a few come to know themselves only through failures and disappointments. Strangers to their own defects—perhaps also to their own powers—they see how they might have succeeded only when success is finally forfeited. Their eyes open too late. A Southern orator tells of a little colored lad who very much wished to have a kitten from a newborn litter, and whose mistress promised that, as soon as they wer old enough, he should take one. Too impatient to wait, he slyly carried one off to his hut. Its eyes were not open, and, in disgust, he drowned it. But, subsequently finding the kitten lying in the pail dead, but with open eyes, he exclaimed, "Umph! When you's alive, you's blind. Now you's dead, you see!" It will be a real calamity to us if our eyes only open when it is too late to make our life of any use.

All true life-power has a basis of high *moral integrity*. Far higher in the scale than any life of impulse, passion, or even opinion, is the life regulated by principle. The end of life is something more than pleasure. Man is not a piece of vitalized sponge, to absorb all into himself. The essentials of happiness are something to love, something to hope for, something to do—affection, aspiration, action.

We must also educate our dispositions. Some one has said: "Disposition is a lens through which men and things are seen. A fiery temper, like a red glass, gives to all objects a lurid glare; a melancholic temper, like a blue lens, imparts its own hue; through the green spectacles of jealousy every one else becomes an object of distrust and dislike; and he who looks through the black glass of malice, finds others wearing the aspect of his own malevolence. Only the cheerful and charitable soul sees through a clear and colorless medium, whose transparency shows the world as it is."

Disposition has also its concave and convex lenses, which magnify some things and minify others. The self-satisfied man sees every one's faults in giant proportions; and every one's virtues, but his own, dwarfed into insignificance. To the fretful man others seem fretful; to the envious man, envious; and so with the well-disposed, gentle, and generous; sunshine prevails over shadows. The world is different to different observers, largely because they have different media through which they look at it.

Cheerful tempers manufacture solace and joy out of very unpromising material. They are the magic alchemists who extract sweet essences out of bitter herbs, like the old colored woman in the smoky hut, who was "glad of anything to make a smoke with," and, though she had but two teeth, thanked God they were "*opposite each other!*"

Goodness outranks even uprightness, because the good man aims to do good to others. Uprightness is the beauty of integrity; goodness is the loveliness of benevolence. The good man visits the hut of misery, the hovel of poverty, leaving in a gentle and delicate way, a few comforts for the table or wardrobe, dainties for the fevered palate of the sick, or such other helps as the case may call for, as far as his means and circumstances will allow.

A true education should cover all these points, and many others also; but it must never be allowed to destroy the pupil's individuality. It must teach that a person can be himself, and study all the models he pleases. Webster studied the orations of Cicero so thoroughly that he could repeat most of them by heart; but they did not destroy or compromise his individuality, because he did not try to be Cicero. It has been said that Michael Angelo, who was the most original of ancient or modern artists, was more familiar with the model statues and paintings of the world than any other man. He studied the excellences of all the great works of art, not to copy or imitate them, but to develop his powers. "As the food he consumed became bone and muscle by assimilation; so, by mental assimilation, the knowledge he acquired by art-models entered into the very composition of his mind."

The more thoroughly a man's nature is developed under the influences of a good education, the more justly does he claim the liberty of thought and action, and a suitable field whereon to think and act. The materials of useful and honorable life—of life aiming at great and noble ends—are within him. He feels it, he knows it to be so; and a denial uttered by ten thousand voices would not check the ardor of his pursuit, or induce him to surrender one atom of his claim. His claim involves a right. He is as conscious of it as of his existence. His mind has acquired the power of observing, reasoning, reflecting, judging, and acting; and he feels that, like a pendulum, the action of his mind is capable of giving activity, force, and value, to a large body of well-compacted machinery, of which he is a part.

It is the mind that acts as the universal pendulum; and if its liberty of action be circumscribed, and its vibrations consequently fall short of the mark, then its power will be crippled, and the life, as a whole will be imperfect and incomplete.

II.

OBSERVATION.

MEMORY GEMS.

We get out of Nature what we carry to her.—Katherine Hagar

Fools learn nothing from wise men, but wise men learn much from fools.
—Lavater

The non-observant man goes through the forest and sees no firewood.
—Russian Proverb

Some men will learn more in a country stage-ride than others in a tour
of Europe.—Dr. Johnson

The world is full of thoughts, and you will find them strewed
everywhere in your path.—Elihu Burritt

All conscious life begins in observation. We say of a baby, "See how he *notices!*" By this statement we really call attention to the fact that the child is beginning to be interested in things separate from and outside of himself. Up to this time he has *seen* but not *observed*, for to observe is to "see with attention"; to "notice with care"; to see with the mind as well as with the eye. There are many persons who see almost everything but observe almost nothing. They are forever fluttering over the surface of things, but put forth no real effort to secure and preserve the ideas they ought to gather from the scenes through which they pass.

Every boy and girl in the land, possessing a good pair of eyes, has the means for acquiring a vast store of knowledge. As the child, long before he can talk, obtains a pretty good idea of the little world that lies within his vision; so may all bright, active boys and girls obtain, by correct habits of observation, a knowledge that will the better fit them for the active duties of manhood and womanhood.

The active, observing eye is the sign of intelligence; while the vacant, listless stare of indifference betokens an empty brain. The eyes are placed in an elevated position that they may better observe all that comes within their range. These highways to the soul should always stand wide open, ready to carry inward all such impressions as will add to our knowledge.

No object the eye ever beholds, no sound, however slight, caught by the ear, or anything once passing the turnstile of any of the senses, is ever again let go. The eye is a perpetual camera, imprinting upon the sensitive mental plates, and packing away in the brain for future use, every face, every plant and flower, every scene upon the street, in fact, everything which comes within its range. It should, therefore, be easy to discern that since mere seeing may create false impressions in the mind, and that only by careful observation can we gather for future use such impressions as are thoroughly reliable, we cannot well overestimate the importance of its cultivation.

It is beyond question that childhood and early youth are the most favorable periods for the cultivation of this faculty. Not only is the mind then more free from care, and, therefore, more at leisure to observe, but it is also more easy to interest one's self in the common things, which, while they lie nearest to us, make up by far the greater portion of our lives. Experience also proves that a person is not a good observer at the age of twenty, in ninety-nine cases out of a hundred he will never become one. "The student," says Hugh Miller, "should learn to make a right use of his eyes; the commonest things are worth looking at; even the stones and weeds, and the most familiar animals. Then in early manhood he is prepared to study men and things in a way to make success easy and sure."

Houdin, the magician, spent a month in cultivating the observing powers of his son. Together they walked rapidly past the window of a large toy store. Then each would write down the things that he had seen. The boy soon became so expert that one glance at a show window would enable him to write down the names of forty different objects. The boy could easily outdo his father.

The power of observation in the American Indian would put many an educated white man to shame. Returning home, an Indian discovered that his venison, which had been hanging up to dry, had been stolen. After careful observation he started to track the thief through the woods. Meeting a man on the route, he asked him if he had seen a little, old, white man, with a short gun, and with a small bob-tailed dog. The man told him he had met such a man, but was surprised to find that the Indian had not even seen the one he described. He asked the Indian how he could give such a minute description of a man whom he had never seen.

"I knew the thief was a little man," said the Indian, "because he rolled up a stone to stand on in order to reach the venison; I knew he was an old man by his short steps; I knew he was a white man by his turning out his toes in walking, which an Indian never does; I knew he had a short gun by the mark it left on the tree where he had stood it up; I knew the dog was small by his tracks and short steps, and that he had a bob-tail by the mark it left in the dust where he sat."

The poet Longfellow has also dwelt upon the power of observation in the early training of Hiawatha. You will perhaps recall the lines:

"Then the little Hiawatha
Learned of every bird its language,
Learned their names and all their secrets,
How they built their nests in summer,
Where they hid themselves in winter,
Talked with them whene'er he met them,
Called them 'Hiawatha's Chickens.'"

The most noted men of every land and age have acquired their fame by carrying into effect ideas suggested by or obtained from observation.

The head of a large commercial firm was once asked why he employed such an ignorant man for a buyer. He replied: "It is true that our buyer cannot spell correctly; but when anything comes within the range of his eyes, he sees all that there is to be seen. He buys over a million dollars' worth a year for us, and I cannot recall any instance when he failed to notice a defect in any line of goods or any feature that would be likely to render them unsalable." This man's highly developed power of observation was certainly of great value.

Careful observers become accurate thinkers. These are the men that are needed everywhere and by everybody. By observation the scholar gets more out of his books, the traveler more enjoyment from the beauties of nature, and the young person who is quick to read human character avoids companions that would be likely to lead him into the ways of vice and folly, and perhaps cause his life to become a total wreck.

JOHN JAMES AUDUBON.

In 1828 a wonderful book, "The Birds of America," by John James Audubon, was issued. It is a good illustration of what has been accomplished by beginning in one's youth to use the powers of observation. Audubon loved and studied birds. Even in his infancy, lying under the orange trees on his father's plantation in Louisiana, he listened to the mocking bird's song, watching and observing every motion as it flitted from bough to bough. When he was older he began to sketch every bird that he saw, and soon showed so much talent that he was taken to France to be educated.

He entered cheerfully and earnestly upon his studies, and more than a year was devoted to mathematics; but whenever it was possible he rambled about the country, using his eyes and fingers, collecting more specimens, and sketching with such assiduity that when he left France, only seventeen years old, he had finished two hundred drawings of French birds. At this period he tells us that "it was not the desire of fame which prompted to this devotion; it was simply the enjoyment of nature."

A story is told of his lying on his back in the woods with some moss for his pillow, and looking through a telescopic microscope day after day to watch a pair of little birds while they made their nest. Their peculiar grey plumage harmonized with the color of the bark of the tree, so that it was impossible to see the birds except by the most careful observation. After three weeks of such patient labor, he felt that he had been amply rewarded for the toil and sacrifice by the results he had obtained.

His power of observation gave him great happiness, from the time he rambled as a boy in the country in search of treasures of natural history, till, in his old age, he rose with the sun and went straightway to the woods near his home, enjoying still the beauties and wonders of Nature. His strength of purpose and unwearied energy, combined with his pure enthusiasm, made him successful in his work as a naturalist; but it was all dependent on the habit formed in his boyhood,—this habit of close and careful observation; and he not only had this habit of using his eyes, but he looked at and studied things worth seeing, worth remembering.

This brief sketch of Audubon's boyhood shows the predominant traits of his character,—his power of observation, the training of the eye and hand, that made him in manhood "the most distinguished of American ornithologists," with so much scientific ardor and perseverance that no expedition seemed dangerous, or solitude inaccessible, when he was engaged in his favorite study.

He has left behind him, as the result of his labors, his great book on "The Birds of America," in ten volumes; and illustrated with four hundred and forty-eight colored plates of over one thousand species of birds, all drawn by his own hand, and each bird being represented in its natural size; also a "Biography of American Birds," in five large volumes, in which he describes their habits and customs. He was associated with Dr. Bachman of Philadelphia, in the preparation of a work on "The Quadrupeds of America," in six large volumes, the drawings for which were made by his two sons; and, later on, published his "Biography of American Quadrupeds," a work similar to the "Biography of the Birds." He died at what is known as "Audubon Park," on the Hudson, now within the limits of New York city, in 1851, at the age of seventy.

[Footnote: For fuller information concerning Audubon, consult "Life and Adventures of John J. Audubon," by Robert Buchanan (New York, 1869); Griswold's "Prose Writers of America" (Philadelphia, 1847); Mrs. Horace St. John's "Audubon the Naturalist" (New York, 1856); Rev. C. C. Adams's "Journal of the Life and Labors of J. J. Audubon" (Boston, 1860), and "Audubon and his Journals," by M. R. Audubon (New York, 1897).]

III.

OBEDIENCE.

MEMORY GEMS.

Love makes obedience easy.—T. Watson

The education of the will is the object of our existence.—Emerson

To learn obeying is the fundamental art of governing.—Carlyle

True obedience neither procrastinates nor questions.—Francis Quarles

If thou wouldst be obeyed as a father, be obedient as a son.
—William Penn

By obedience is meant submission to authority, and to proper restraint and control. It is the doing of that which we are told to do; and the refraining from that which is forbidden. At its very best it may be defined as the habit of yielding willingly to command or restraint.

As observation forms the first step in the culture of the mind, so obedience forms the first step in the building of the character. It is as important to the life as is the foundation to the house. Thomas Carlyle has well said that "Obedience is our universal duty and destiny, wherein whosoever will not bend must break." It is impossible to escape from it altogether, and it is therefore wise to learn to obey as early in life as possible.

It does not take very long for a child to learn that it cannot do everything that it would like to do. The wishes of others must be regarded. These wishes spring from a knowledge of what is best. Children, with their limited experiences, cannot always foresee the consequences of their doings. For their own good they must not be allowed to do anything that would result in harm to themselves or to others. Some one must oversee and direct them until they can act intelligently. Obedience is one of the principal laws of the family. The harmony and peace of the entire household depend upon it.

True obedience does not argue nor dispute; neither does it delay nor murmur. It goes directly to work to fulfil the commands laid upon us, or to refrain from doing that which is forbidden. "Sir," said the Duke of Wellington to an officer of engineers, who urged the impossibility of executing his orders, "I did not ask your opinion. I gave you my orders, and I expect them to be obeyed."

A story is told of a great captain, who, after a battle, was talking over the events of the day with his officers. He asked them who had done the best that day. Some spoke of one man who had fought very bravely, and some of another. "No," said he, "you are all mistaken. The best man in the field to-day was a soldier, who was just lifting his arm to strike an enemy, but when he heard the trumpet sound a retreat, checked himself, and dropped his arm without striking a blow. That perfect and ready obedience to the will of his general, is the noblest thing that has been done to-day."

The instant obedience of the child is as beautiful and as important as that of the soldier. The unhesitating obedience which springs from a loving confidence is beautifully illustrated in the following incident: A switchman in Prussia was stationed at the junction of two lines of railroad. His hand was on the lever for a train that was approaching. The engine was within a few seconds of reaching his signal box when, on turning his head, the switchman saw his little boy playing on the line of rails over which the train was to pass. "Lie down!" he shouted to the child; but, he himself, remained at his post. The train passed safely on its way. The father rushed forward, expecting to take up a corpse; but what was his joy on finding that the boy had obeyed his order so promptly that the whole train had passed over him without injury. The next day the king sent for the man and attached to his breast the medal for civil courage.

A cheerful obedience is one of the strongest proofs of love. "Love is to obedience like wings to the bird, or sails to the ship. It is the agency that carries it forward to success. When love cools, obedience slackens; and nothing is worthy of the name of love that leads to disobedience."

We remember the anecdote of a Roman commander, who forbade an engagement with the enemy, and the first transgressor was his own son. He accepted the challenge of the leader of the other host, slew and disrobed him, and then in triumph carried the spoils to his father's tent. But the Roman father refused to recognize the instinct which prompted this, as deserving the name of love.

Many of the restraints laid upon us result from the love of those in authority. If we were permitted to pursue our own inclinations, our health might be destroyed, our minds run to waste, and we should be apt to grow up slothful and selfish; a trouble to others and burdensome to ourselves. It is far easier to obey our parents and friends when we recall that we have experienced their goodness long enough to know that they wish to make us happy, even when their commands seem most severe. Let us, therefore, show our appreciation of their goodness by doing cheerfully what they require.

The will is supported, strengthened, and perfected by obedience. There are many who suppose that real strength of will is secured by giving it free play. But we really weaken it in that way. Obedience to a reasonable law is a source of moral strength and power. Obedience is not weakness bowing to strength, but is rather submission to an authority whose claims are already admitted. If a man is royal when he rules over nature, and yet more royal when he rules his brother man, is he not most royal when he so rules himself as to do the right even when it is distasteful?

A man who had declared his aversion for what he called the dry facts of political economy, was found one day knitting his brows over a book on that subject. When a friend expressed surprise, the man replied: "I am playing the schoolmaster with myself. I am reading this because I dislike it."

Difficulties are often really helpful. They enlarge our experience and incite us to do our best. "The head of Hercules," says Ruskin, "was always represented as covered with a lion's skin, with the claws joining under the chin, to show that when we had conquered our misfortunes they became a help to us."

One of the greatest hindrances to obedience is a false pride. The thought of living under the will and direction of another is exceedingly unpleasant, and where such a pride bears rule in the heart, a cheerful obedience is almost an impossibility. We often fail to obey simply because we are unwilling to acknowledge ourselves in the wrong.

Obedience is also hindered by ignorance. One of our commonest errors is that which teaches that authority is always pleasant, and submission always painful. The actual experiences of life prove that the place of command is usually a position of great anxiety, while the place of obedience is generally one of ease and freedom from care.

Indolence also opposes obedience. In our selfish love of ease we allow duties to go undone until the habit of disobedience becomes almost unnoticeable; but when we find ourselves compelled to resist it, we then discover that to break away from its power is one of the hardest tasks we can be called upon to perform.

THE CHARGE OF THE LIGHT BRIGADE.

A very striking example of prompt and unquestioning obedience is furnished us in that famous "Charge of the Light Brigade" at Balaclava, during the Crimean War, of which you have all doubtless heard. A series of engagements between the Russians on the one side, and the English and their allies on the other side, took place near this little town, on October 25, 1854. The Russians were for a time victorious, and at last threatened the English port of Balaclava itself. The attack was diverted by a brilliant charge of the Heavy Brigade, led by General Scarlett. Then, through a misunderstanding of the orders of Lord Raglan, the commander-in-chief, Lord Cardigan was directed to charge the Russian artillery at the northern extremity of the Balaclava valley with the Light Brigade, then under his command.

Lord Cardigan was an exceedingly unpopular officer, and greatly disliked by all his men, But no sooner was the order given than, with a battery in front of them, and one on either side, the Light Brigade hewed its way past these deadly engines of war and routed the enemy's cavalry. Of the six hundred and seventy horsemen who made the charge, only one hundred and ninety-eight returned. As an act of war it was madness. In the opinion of the most competent judges there was no good end to be gained by it. But as an act of soldierly obedience it was sublime. The deed has been immortalized by the poet Tennyson in the following verses:

I.
Half a league, half a league,
Half a league onward,
All in the valley of Death
 Rode the six hundred.
"Forward, the Light Brigade!
Charge for the guns!" he said:
Into the valley of Death
 Rode the six hundred.

II.
"Forward, the Light Brigade!"
Was there a man dismay'd?
Not tho' the soldier knew
 Some one had blunder'd:
Theirs not to make reply,
Theirs not to reason why,
Theirs but to do and die:
Into the valley of Death
 Rode the six hundred.

III.
Cannon to right of them,
Cannon to left of them,
Cannon in front of them
 Volley'd and thunder'd;
Storm'd at with shot and shell
Boldly they rode and well,
Into the jaws of Death,
Into the mouth of Hell
 Rode the six hundred.

IV.
Flash'd all their sabers bare,
Flash'd as they turn'd in air
Sabring the gunners there,
Charging an army, while

All the world wonder'd:
Plunged in the battery-smoke,
Right thro' the line they broke;
Cossack and Russian
Reel'd from the saber-stroke
 Shattered and sunder'd.
Then they rode back, but not
 Not the six hundred.

V.
Cannon to right of them,
Cannon to left of them,
Cannon behind them
 Volley'd and thunder'd;
Storm'd at with shot and shell,
While horse and hero fell,
They that had fought so well
Came thro' the jaws of Death
Back from the mouth of Hell,
All that was left of them,
 Left of six hundred.

VI.
When can their glory fade?
O the wild charge they made!
 All the world wonder'd.
Honor the charge they made!
Honor the Light Brigade,
 Noble six hundred!

[Footnote: For the story of the Crimean War, consult "Encyclopedia Britannica", Vol. VIII., p. 366; also Vol. XVII., pp. 228 and 486.]

IV.

CANDOR.

MEMORY GEMS.

Truth lies at the bottom of the well.—Old Proverb

Candor looks with equal fairness at both sides of a subject.
    —Noah Webster

Daylight and truth meet us with clear dawn.—Milton

Perfect openness is the only principle on which a free people can be
    governed.—C. B. Yonge

There is no fear for any child who is frank with his father and
    mother.—Buskin

Candor and frankness are so closely akin to each other that we may properly study them together. Each of these words has an interesting origin. "Candor" comes from a Latin word meaning "*to be white*"; while "frankness" is derived from the name of the Franks, who were a powerful German tribe honorably distinguished for their love of freedom and their scorn of a lie. A candid man is one who is disposed to think and judge according to truth and justice, and without partiality or prejudice; while the one word *frank* is used to express anything that is generous, straightforward and free.

Candor is a virtue which is everywhere commended, though not quite so prevalent in the world as might be expected. There are doctors who never tell a patient they can make nothing of his case, or that it is one which requires the attention of a specialist. There are lawyers who never assure a client that it is hopeless for him to expect to gain his suit. And so, in all trades and professions, candor is as rare as it is good.

The lack of a simple and straightforward statement of such facts as are in our possession, often leads to serious misunderstanding and sometimes to serious loss.

Frankness is a combination of truthfulness and courage. Its usefulness depends largely on its association with other qualities and circumstances; but to be frank is simply to dare to be truthful. There are many men who would scorn to tell a lie, who are destitute of frankness because they hesitate to face the consequences of perfect openness of speech or conduct.

An Irishman, who had neglected to thatch his cottage, was one day asked by a gentleman with whom he was conversing, "Did it rain yesterday?" Instead of making a direct and candid reply, he sought to hide his fault, which he supposed had been discovered; and the conversation proceeded as follows.

"Did it rain yesterday?" asked his friend. "Is it yesterday you mean?" was the reply. "Yes, yesterday." "Please your honor, I wasn't at the bog at all yesterday,—wasn't I after setting my potatoes?" "My good friend, I don't know what you mean about the bog; I only asked you whether it rained yesterday?" "Please your honor, I couldn't get a car and horse any way, to draw home my little straw, or I'd have the house thatched long ago." "Cannot you give me a plain answer to this plain question—Did it rain yesterday?" "Oh sure, I wouldn't go to tell your honor a lie about the matter. Sorrah much it rained yesterday after twelve o'clock, barring a few showers." Of course there will be no difficulty in seeing that such a conversation could not be entirely satisfactory to either party.

The virtue we are now recommending is in daily and hourly demand, and of high and priceless value. But here also we must beware of counterfeits. A smooth outward manner, a countenance clothed with perpetual smiles, and an address distinguished by gentleness and insinuation, may be assumed for selfish ends. A truly candid man is neither carried away by ungenerous suspicion, nor by a weak acceptance of the views of others; and the whole constitution of his mind must be entirely changed before he can become capable of deceit.

Frankness has often been counterfeited by mere *bluster*. A couple of striking examples of this fact are brought into view in the recently published "Life and Letters of Charles Darwin," in which, speaking of his childhood, Mr. Darwin says: "One little event has fixed itself very firmly in my mind, and I hope it has done so from my conscience having been afterward sorely troubled by it. It is curious as showing that apparently I was interested at this early age in the variability of plants! I told another little boy that I could produce variously colored primroses by watering them with certain colored fluids, which was of course a monstrous fable, and has never been tried by me. I may here also confess that as a little boy I was much given to inventing deliberate falsehoods, and this was always done for the sake of causing excitement. For instance, I once gathered much valuable fruit from my father's trees and hid it in the shrubbery, and then ran in breathless haste to spread the news that I had discovered a hoard of stolen fruit."

Mr. Darwin also relates the following incident, as illustrating the lack of truthfulness and candor on the part of another: "I must have been a very simple fellow when I first went to school. A boy of the name of Garnett took me into a cake shop one day, and bought some cakes for which he did not pay, as the shopman trusted him. When we came out I asked him why he did not pay for them, and he instantly answered, 'Why, do you not know that my uncle left a great sum of money to the town on condition that every tradesman should give whatever was wanted without payment to any one who wore his old hat and moved it in a particular manner?' He then showed me how to move the hat, and said, 'Now, if you would like to go yourself into that cake shop, I will lend you my hat, and you can get whatever you like if you move the hat on your head properly.' I gladly accepted the generous offer, and went in and asked for some cakes, moved the old hat, and was walking out of the shop, when the shopman made a rush at me; so I dropped the cakes and ran for dear life, and was astonished by being greeted with shouts of laughter by my false friend Garnett." The same truth is illustrated in the case of an affected young lady who, on being asked, in a large company, if she had read Shakespeare, assumed a look of astonishment and replied: "Read Shakespeare! Of course I have! I read that when it first came out!"

Frankness and candor will always win respect and friendship, and will always retain them; and the consciousness of having such a treasure, and of being worthy of it, is more than wealth and honors. A man quickly finds when he is unworthy of public respect or private friendship; and the leaden weight he carries ever in his heart, cannot be lightened by any success or any gratification he may secure. But the man of upright character, and proper self-respect, will never meet with such trials as can deprive him of that higher happiness which rests in his own breast.

True candor is manly and leads directly to the development of nobility both of principle and conduct. The late Hon. William P. Fessenden once made a remark which was understood as an insult to Mr. Seward. When informed of it, and seeing such a meaning could be given to his words, he instantly went to Mr. Seward, and said, "Mr. Seward, I have insulted you: I am sorry for it. I did not mean it." This apology, so prompt, frank, and perfect, so delighted Mr. Seward, that, grasping him by the hand, he exclaimed, "God bless you, Fessenden! I wish you would insult me again!" Such an exhibition of real manliness as this may well be cited as worthy of the imitation of the youth of the land.

DEAN STANLEY.

In "Tom Brown's Schooldays," that charming book, so dear to all wide-awake boys, there is a scene in which little Arthur is introduced in the act of kneeling beside his bed, on his first night at school, for the purpose of saying his prayers according to the custom he had always observed at his home. We are not so much concerned with the fact that he was ridiculed and persecuted by the older boys, as with the further factthat this boy Arthur is said to bear a remarkable resemblance to Arthur Penrhyn Stanley, whose name is everywhere known as the late Dean of Westminster Abbey, the most famous church in England, if not of the world at large. Arthur Stanley was one of the first boys to go to Rugby after the great Dr. Arnold took charge of the school, and an early illustration of his candor and open-mindedness is shown in his immediate and public appreciation of the splendid qualities of his master, at a time when Dr. Arnold was so generally abused, and even branded as an infidel. Dr. Arnold was indeed a noble teacher, and the very man to develop the best faculties in young Arthur Stanley; for one of the doctor's own strongest traits was this same open-mindedness. The frankness and candor, the directness and fearlessness with which Stanley ever gave expression to his views; the purity and "whiteness" of his mind, and the sweetness and tenderness of his disposition,—all these had a part in the building of his fame. But it was chiefly in his power to free himself from prejudice and to look fairly at all sides of the complex questions with which both he and the church to which he belonged were so frequently brought face to face, that gave him his great popular influence, and made him so great a champion of religious liberty. Truth, simplicity and innocence are three jewels which many men barter for worldly honor and success; but Stanley held to these as with a grip of steel; and, through their influence, he succeeded where a score of the great men of his day had already failed.

To tell of all that candor and frankness have done for humanity would be to trace the beginnings of the overthrow of almost every wrong. Other qualities are of course essential to all noble reformers—courage and faith and enthusiasm; but open-mindedness, which grows out of candor and frankness, is the one pioneer that recognizes the opportunity of the hour and is willing to walk in the new light. Candor is the sign of a noble mind. It is the pride of the true man, the charm of the noble woman, the defeat and mockery of the hypocrite, and the rarest virtue of society.

[Footnote: An admirable sketch of the career of Dean Stanley will be found in Johnson's Universal Cyclopedia, Vol. VII., p. 697. See also "Life of Dean Stanley," by R. E. Prothero (London and New York, 1894).]

V.

AFFECTION.

MEMORY GEMS.

Gratitude is the music of the heart.—Robert South.

The best way of recognizing a benefit is never to forget it.
—J. J. Barthelmey

The affection and the reason are both necessary factors in morality.
—Fowler

True love burns hottest when the weather is coldest.—Swinnock

> The mind has a thousand eyes,
> And the heart but one;
> Yet the light of a whole life dies
> When love is done.—F. W. Bourdillon

One of the most powerful forces in the building of character is affection; and one of the most common forms of its manifestation is gratitude. The exercise of affection makes us tender and loving toward all living persons and creatures about us; while the exercise of gratitude usually results in making them tender and loving toward us.

Every boy and girl should endeavor to cultivate this spirit of affectionate consideration for the feelings of others, and should be careful not to speak any word, or do any act, or even give any look which can cause unnecessary pain. And yet there are many young people, who have never been taught better, who take exceeding pleasure in causing annoyance and even suffering to all with whom they have to do. This is done with the simple idea of having a little fun; but it is one of the worst habits we can possibly form, and should be carefully avoided by all who would command the respect and esteem which every young person should desire to possess.

Perhaps you have heard the story of the youth who, while walking out with his tutor, saw a pair of shoes that a poor laborer had left under a hedge while he was busied with his work. "What fun it would be," exclaimed the young man, "to hide these shoes, and then to conceal ourselves behind the hedge, and see the man's surprise and excitement when he cannot find them." "I will tell you what would be better sport," said the tutor; "put a piece of money into one of the shoes, and then hide and watch his surprise when he finds it." This the young man did; and the joy and wonder of the poor laborer when he found the money in his shoe was as good fun as he wanted.

We all know what the feeling of gratitude is. We have said "Thank you," a great many times; and have often felt really grateful in our hearts for gifts and favors received. But we are too apt to forget that we have any one to thank for the most important benefits of our lives. When we stop to think, we see that all we have done or can do for ourselves is very little indeed in comparison with what has been done for us.

How much we owe to our parents! What other creature in the world is so helpless as the human infant? Leave a little baby to take care of itself, and how long do you suppose it would live? How many of us would be alive to-day, if in our earliest years we had not been provided for and watched over with tender care? But the outward benefits for which children have to thank their parents are of less value than the lessons of truth and goodness which are never so well taught as by the lips of a faithful and devoted father and mother. To these lessons the greatest and best men generally look back with the deepest gratitude.

A child's affection for his parents ought to make him tender toward them when age or disease has made them irritable or complaining. A love that only accepts, and never gives, is not worthy of the name.

Sometimes we hear of old men and women who are left to die alone, whose children have deserted them, and who have no friends in the world. These cases seem pitiful enough, and it breaks our hearts to think of them. But usually the men and women who are left desolate in their old age are those who have been unloving in their youth. "A man that hath friends must show himself friendly," and an aged man or woman who has made friends through life, and been full of love and affection toward others, is tolerably sure to be tenderly cared for in later years. But true affection is never eager for returns. We love because we must love; never because we expect to be loved in return. We do for others because we wish to make them happy; and not because we wish them to do for us.

Kindness and generosity have their place in the playground. There may be thoughtfulness for one who is weaker than the rest, or who is a newcomer, or who, for any reason, is neglected by others. There is an opportunity to stand up for those who are ill-used. There is a generous sympathy for those who, in any way, are having a hard time.

In all these ways boys and girls, when they are at play, show pretty well what they are going to be in later life. When Napoleon was at a military school, the boys were one day playing at war. One set of them held a fort which the others were trying to capture. The boy, Napoleon, led the attacking party. In the midst of the fight there was a flourish of trumpets, and a party of officers entered, who had come to inspect the school. The boys that held the fort forgot their play, and stood staring at the entering group. Napoleon did not lose his head for a moment. He kept his party up to their work. He took advantage of the interruption, and when the besieged recovered their wits, their fort was captured. He was already the Napoleon who in the real battles of later years knew how to turn so many seemingly adverse circumstances to good account.

We always think of Sir Walter Scott as a very affectionate man; but once when he was a boy he saw a dog coming toward him and carelessly threw a stone at him. The stone broke the dog's leg. The poor creature had strength to crawl up to him and lick his feet. This incident, he afterward said, had given him the bitterest remorse. He never forgot it. From that moment he resolved never to be unkind to any animal. We know that he kept that resolution, for he wrote many of his novels with his faithful dogs Maida, Nimrod, and Bran near him. When Maida died he had a sculptured monument of her set up before his door.

We all know boys who throw stones at animals from pure thoughtlessness and love of fun. But no boy with a really affectionate nature can bear to make an animal or a human being suffer pain. A boy who begins by being cruel to animals usually ends by being cruel to women and children. A girl who habitually forgets to feed her kitten or her canary birds, will be apt to forget her child later in life.

Half a century ago there lived in the state of Massachusetts a very remarkable man named Thoreau. This man became so deeply interested in the animal world that he built a little hut for himself near Walden pond, and he there lived in the closest sympathy with the birds and animals for more than two years. It is said that even the snakes loved him, and would wind round his legs; and on taking a squirrel from a tree the little creature would hide its head in his waistcoat. The fish in the river knew him and would let him lift them out of the water, and the little wood-mice came and nibbled at the cheese he held in his hand. It was Thoreau's love for the little wild creatures which drew them to him, for animals are as responsive to love as are human beings.

John Howard gave his life to the work of improving the condition of prisons all over the world, and finally he died alone in Russia of jail fever. He was followed in his labors by Elizabeth Fry in England, and by Dorothea Dix in America. These noble philanthropists were filled with unselfish love toward suffering humanity. They devoted their lives to the neglected and forsaken, including the whole world in their generous hearts; and their names and deeds will never be forgotten.

There are two principal ways in which our kindly feelings may be made known: First, *in our words*. It is pleasant to those who do us favors to know that we appreciate their kindness, and we should never fail to tell them so. This is often all the return that they expect or ask; besides, it is good for us.

We strengthen our feelings by giving them suitable expression. Loveless at last is the home in which no word of love is ever heard. The grateful feeling to which one gives utterance kindles the same feeling in the hearts of those who hear.

Second, *in our deeds*. If we are really grateful we are not satisfied with simply saying, "Thank you," to those who have been kind to us, even when we know this is all they expect. We wish to render them some service in return. In the case of our parents, as long as they are with us, we can best do this by doing cheerfully what they ask us to do, by thoughtfully anticipating their wishes, and by trying to be as pure and good as we know they want us to be.

ABRAHAM LINCOLN.

Abraham Lincoln was a poor boy. His early life was full of hardships; but many a kind friend helped him in his struggle against poverty. Among these friends of his early youth was one, Jack Armstrong, of New Salem, Illinois, whose kind, good-hearted wife performed for Lincoln many a motherly act of kindness. She made his clothes and "got him something to eat while he rocked the baby." Years passed by. Lincoln became a successful lawyer. Soon after he had entered upon the practice of his profession at Springfield, his old friend, Jack Armstrong died. The baby whom Lincoln had rocked grew into a stout but dissolute young man. He was arrested, charged with the crime of murder. "Aunt Hannah," as Lincoln used to call her, was heartbroken with sorrow for her poor, misguided boy. In her grief she appealed to the "noble, good Abe," who had rocked her son when he was a baby. The appeal brought tears to the eyes of Lincoln. His generous heart was touched. He resolved to discharge the debt of gratitude which neither his great success in life nor the intervening years had erased from his memory. He pledged his services without charge.

"Aunt Hannah" believed that her boy was innocent and that others wished to fasten the crime upon him because of his bad reputation. The circumstances of the case were as follows: While Armstrong was in the company of several fast young men, they became intoxicated. A "free fight" ensued in which a young fellow named Metzgar was killed. After hearing the facts, Lincoln was convinced that the young man was not guilty, and resolved to do his best to save him from the gallows.

Lincoln secured a postponement of the trial and spent much time in tracing the evidence. He labored as hard to pay his old debt of gratitude as he would have done if he had been offered a five thousand dollar fee.

The day for the trial came. Lincoln threw his whole soul into the effort to defend the life of his client. He succeeded in proving his innocence beyond the shadow of a doubt. The closing of his plea was a marvel of eloquence.

He depicted the loneliness and sorrow of the widowed mother, whose husband had once welcomed to his humble home a strange and penniless boy. "That boy now stands before you pleading for the life of his benefactor's son."

When the jury brought in the verdict, "not guilty," a shout of joy went up from the crowded court room. The aged mother pressed forward through the throng and, with tears streaming from her eyes, attempted to express to Lincoln her gratitude for his noble effort.

Some months afterward Lincoln called to see her at her home. She urged him to take pay for his services. "Why, Aunt Hannah," he exclaimed, "I shan't take a cent of yours; never! Anything I can do for you, I will willingly, and without any charge."

True gratitude never forgets. No one can possess too much gratitude any more than he can have too much honesty or truthfulness. It was a "pearl of great price" in Lincoln's heart. He was truer and nobler for it; and it did much to endear him to the American people, by whom he is still remembered as one of the most large-hearted and liberal-minded men our country has produced.

[Footnote: See also biographies of Lincoln, by Holland (1865); Arnold (1868); Lamon (1872); Nicolay and Hay (1890); Schurz (1892); and Herndon (1892, revised edition).]

VI.

CHEERFULNESS.

MEMORY GEMS.

Cheerfulness is the best promoter of health.—Addison

Give us, oh give us, the man who sings at his work.—Carlyle

Age without cheerfulness is like a Lapland winter without the sun.
—Colton

An ounce of cheerfulness is worth a pound of sadness.—Fuller

The habit of looking at the bright side of things is better than an income of a thousand a year.—Hume.

We all love the company of cheerful people, but we do not think, as much as we ought to, of the nature of cheerfulness itself. Because we find that some people are naturally cheerful, we are apt to forget that cheerfulness is a habit which can be cultivated by all. Whether we do or do not possess a cheerful disposition, depends very largely upon our own efforts; for if we will endeavor, while still in our early years, to form the habit of looking on the bright side of things, and then persist in this course as we grow older, we shall certainly attain to that habitual cheerfulness which makes the lives of those we admire so sunny and so pleasing.

Even the smallest matters may aid us in forming this habit. Perhaps you have heard of the little girl who noticed, while eating her dinner, that the golden rays of the sun fell upon her spoon. She put the spoon to her mouth, and then exclaimed, "O mother! I have swallowed a whole spoonful of sunshine." Some children even take a cheerful view of their punishments, as seen in the following incident. "Little Charley had been very naughty, and was imprisoned for an hour in the kitchen wood-box. He speedily began amusing himself with chips and splinters, and was playing quite busily and happily, when a neighbor entered the house by way of the kitchen. 'Charley,' he cried, 'what are you doing there?' 'Nothing,' said Charley, 'nothing; but mamma's just been having one of her bad spells.'"

Cheerfulness consists in that happy frame of mind which is best described as the shutting out of all that pertains to the morbid, the gloomy, the fretful, and the discontented. The perfection of cheerfulness is displayed in general good temper united to much kindliness of heart. It arises partly from personal goodness, and partly from belief in the goodness of others. Its face is ever directed toward happiness. It sees "the glory in the grass, the sunshine on the flower." It encourages happy thoughts, and lives in an atmosphere of peace.

It costs nothing, and yet is invaluable; for it blesses its possessor, and affords a large measure of enjoyment to others.

Cheerfulness bears the same friendly regard to the mind as to the body. It banishes all anxious care and discontent, soothes and composes the passions, and keeps the soul in a perpetual calm. Try for a single day to keep yourself in an easy and cheerful frame of mind; and then compare the day with one which has been marred by discontent, and you will find your heart open to every good motive, and your life so greatly strengthened, that you will wonder at your own improvement, and will feel that you are more than repaid for the effort.

Goethe once said, "Give me the man who bears a heavy load lightly, and looks on a grave matter with a blithe and cheerful eye." And Carlyle has pointed out that "One is scarcely sensible of fatigue whilst he marches to music. The very stars are said to make harmony as they revolve in their spheres. Wondrous is the strength of cheerfulness; altogether past calculation its power of endurance. Efforts, to be permanently useful, must be uniformly joyous—a spirit all sunshine, graceful from very gladness, beautiful because bright."

This spirit of cheerfulness should be encouraged in our youth if we would wish to have the benefit of it in our old age. Persons who are always innocently cheerful and good-humored are very useful in the world; they maintain peace and happiness, and spread a thankful temper among all who live around them.

"A little word in kindness spoken
  A motion or a tear,
 Has often healed a heart that's broken,
  And made a friend sincere."

Cheerfulness does not depend upon the measure of our possessions. There is a Persian story to the effect that the great king, being out of spirits, consulted his astrologers, and was told that happiness could be found by wearing the shirt of a perfectly happy man. The court, and the homes of all the prosperous classes were searched in vain; no such man could be found. At last a common laborer was found to fulfill the conditions; he was absolutely happy; but, alas! the remedy was as far off as ever, for the man had no shirt.

The same truth may be illustrated by a reference to the life and character of the Roman emperor, Nero. Few persons ever had greater means and opportunities for self-gratification. From the senator to the slave, everybody in the empire crouched in servile subjection before his throne. Enormous revenues from the provinces were poured into his coffers, and no one dared criticise his manner of spending them. He was absolute monarch, holding the destinies of millions at his will. He came to the throne at seventeen; and during the fifteen years of his reign he exhausted every known means of passionate indulgence. He left nothing untried or untouched that could stimulate the palate, or arouse his passions, or administer in any way to his pleasure. After the great fire in Rome, he built his golden palace, and said, "Now at last I am lodged like a man"; but alas! his search for happiness was in vain. During his later years he never knew a really cheerful day; and, at last, he was forced to flee before his outraged people, and took refuge in a miserable hut, trembling like a base coward, where, at his own request, a slave did him the favor to end his miserable life.

In one of his famous essays, Addison says, "I have always preferred cheerfulness to mirth. The latter I consider as an act, the former as a habit of the mind. Mirth is like a flash of lightning that breaks through a gloom of clouds, and glitters for a moment; cheerfulness keeps up a kind of daylight in the mind, and fills it with a steady and perpetual serenity."

Cheerfulness and good spirits depend in a great degree upon bodily causes; but much may be done for the promotion of this frame of mind. "Persons subject to low spirits should make the room in which they live as cheerful as possible; hanging up pictures or prints, and filling the odd nooks and corners with beautiful ornaments. A bay window looking upon pleasant objects, and, above all, a large fire whenever the weather will permit, are favorable to good spirits, and the tables near should be strewed with books and pamphlets." "To this," says Sydney Smith, "must be added as much eating and drinking as is consistent with health; and some manual employment for men—as gardening, a carpenter's shop, or a turning-lathe. Women have always manual employment enough, and it is a great source of cheerfulness." For children, fresh air, occupation, and outdoor sports are great helps in overcoming depression and gloom.

SYDNEY SMITH.

There are a few noble natures whose very presence carries sunshine with them wherever they go; a sunshine which means pity for the poor, sympathy for the suffering, help for the unfortunate, and kindness toward all. It is the sunshine, and not the cloud, that colors the flower. There is more virtue in one sunbeam than in a whole hemisphere of cloud and gloom.

A man of this stamp is found in Sydney Smith, an English clergyman and writer of great distinction, who was born in 1771, and died in 1845. His was a sunny temperament. Noted for his wit, he was equally famous for his kindness. He hated injustice; he praised virtue; he pierced humbugs; he laughed away trouble; he preached and lived the gospel of Christian cheerfulness.

Smith helped to found the *Edinburgh Review*, and he advocated putting on the title-page this truthful, too truthful, sentence: "We cultivate literature on a little oatmeal." Poor but happy, this jest is characteristic of the man. His name became known: his society was sought. Macaulay and he were called "the great talkers." He moved to London, and gave lectures on moral philosophy that drew crowds, so that the carriages of fashion blocked the streets. He was the charm of every circle. His pen was always on the side of progress and good fellowship.

At every turn in life he made light of vexations, and never allowed himself or those with him to indulge in morbid ideas, imaginative forebodings, or resentment. This is what he wrote to his daughter: "I am not situated as I should choose; but I am resolved to like it, and to reconcile myself to it; which is more manly than to feign myself above it and send up complaints of being thrown away." One of his favorite expressions was, "Let us glorify the room"; which meant, throw up the shades and let in the sunshine.

The following anecdote will help to show his bright and sparkling disposition: At dinner with a large party of famous men and women, a French scientist annoyed all the rest by loudly arguing for atheism, and proclaimed his belief that there is no God. "Very good soup this," struck in Sydney Smith. "Yes, monsieur, it is excellent," replied the atheist. "Pray, sir," continued Smith, "do you believe in a cook?" The ounce of wit was worth a pound of argument.

He is one of the very few men whose names have been handed down to us by reason of the possession of this gift, and his career should be more fully studied.

[Footnote: See "Wit and Wisdom of Sydney Smith," by Duyckinck (1856); "Memoirs of Sydney Smith" by his daughter, Lady Holland (1855); "Life and Times of Sydney Smith," by Stuart J. Reid (London, 1844).]

VII.

THE LOVE OF THE BEAUTIFUL.
MEMORY GEMS.

The beautiful can never die.—Kingsley

A thing of beauty is a joy forever.—Keats

The love of beauty is an essential part of all healthy human nature.
—Ruskin

The sense of beauty is its own excuse for being.—Dr. Hedge

If eyes were made for seeing,
Then beauty is its own excuse for being.—Emerson

One of the principal objects of the large amount of "nature study" that, within recent years, has been pursued in our public schools, is to develop in the pupils the love of the beautiful. The beautiful in nature and art is that which gives pleasure to the senses. The question might be asked, "Why do some forms and colors please, and others displease?" Yankee fashion, it might be answered by the question, "Why do we like sugar and dislike wormwood?" It is also a fact that cultivated minds derive more pleasure from nature and art than uncultivated minds.

This fact is aptly illustrated by the following remark of a little girl in one of the lower grades of our public schools. Shortly after she had taken up the study of plants and minerals she came to her teacher and said, "Oh! we have a lovely time now when we go up to the reservoir to play. Before we studied about plants and stones, we used to go up there and sit down and look around; but now we find so many beautiful things to look at. We know the plants and stones; and what pleasure it does give us to find a new specimen!" This child's love of the beautiful was being intelligently developed.

Natural beauty is an all-pervading presence. It unfolds into the numberless flowers of spring. It waves in the branches of the trees and the green blades of grass. It haunts the depths of the earth and the sea, and gleams from the hues of the shell and the precious stone. And not only these minute objects, but the ocean, the mountains, the clouds, the heavens, the stars, the rising and setting sun—all overflow with beauty. The universe is its temple; and those men who are alive to it cannot lift their eyes without feeling themselves encompassed with it on every side. This beauty is so precious, the enjoyments it gives are so refined and pure, so congenial to our tenderest and noblest feelings, and so akin to worship, that it is painful to think of the multitude of persons living in the midst of it and yet remaining almost as blind to it as if they were tenants of a dungeon.

All persons should seek to become sufficiently acquainted with the beautiful in nature to secure to themselves the rich fund of happiness which it is so well able to give. There is not a worm we tread upon, nor a rare leaf that dances merrily as it falls before the autumn winds, but has superior claims upon our study and admiration. The child who plucks a rose to pieces, or crushes the fragile form of a fluttering insect, destroys a work which the highest art could not create, nor man's best skilled hand construct.

One of the first forms in which man's idea of the beautiful shaped itself was in architecture. Extremely crude at first, this love for beautiful buildings has been highly developed among civilized nations. Ruskin says, "All good architecture is the expression of national life and character, and is produced by a permanent and eager desire or taste for beauty."

A taste for pictures, merely, is not in itself a moral quality; but the taste for *good* pictures is. A beautiful painting by one of the great artists, a Grecian statue, or a rare coin, or magnificent building, is a good and perfect thing; for it gives constant delight to the beholder.

The absence of the love of nature is not an assured ground of condemnation. Its presence is an invariable sign of goodness of heart, though by no means an evidence of moral practice. In proportion to the degree in which it is felt, will probably be the degree in which nobleness and beauty of character will be attained.

One of our great artists has said, that good taste is essentially a moral quality. To his mind, the first, last, and closest trial question to any living creature is, What do you like? Tell me what you like, and I will tell you what you are.

Let us examine this argument. Suppose you go out into the street and ask the first person you meet what he likes? You happen to accost a man in rags with an unsteady step, who, straightening himself up in a half uncertain way, answers, "A pipe and a quart of beer." You can take a pretty good measure of his character from that answer, can you not? But here comes a little girl, with golden hair and soft, blue eyes. "What do you like, my little girl?" "My canary, and to run among the flowers," is her answer. And you, little boy, with dirty hands and low forehead, "What do you like?" "A chance to hit the sparrows with a stone." When we have secured so much knowledge of their tastes, we really know the character of these persons so well that we do not need to ask any further questions about them.

The man who likes what you like must belong to the same class with you. You may give him a different form of work to do, but as long as he likes the things that you like, and dislikes that which you dislike, he will not be content while employed in an inferior position.

Hearing a young lady highly praised for her beauty, Gotthold asked, "What kind of beauty do you mean? Merely that of the body, or that also of the mind? I see well that you have been looking no further than the sign which Nature displays outside the house, but have never asked for the host who dwells within. Beauty is an excellent gift of God, but many a pretty girl is like the flower called 'the imperial crown,' which is admired for its showy appearance, and despised for its unpleasant odor. Were her mind as free from pride, selfishness, luxury, and levity, as her countenance is from spots and wrinkles, and could she govern her inward inclinations as she does her external carriage, she would have none to match her."

The power to appreciate beauty does not merely increase our sources of happiness,—it enlarges our moral nature too. Beauty calms our restlessness and dispels our cares. Go into the fields or the woods, spend a summer day by the sea or the mountains, and all your little perplexities and anxieties vanish. Listen to sweet music, and your foolish fears and petty jealousies pass away. The beauty of the world helps us to seek and find the beauty of goodness.

The love of the beautiful is an unfailing source of happiness. In his brief life, Regnault, the great painter, had more genuine enjoyment than a score of men of duller perceptions. He had cultivated his sense of color and proportion until nothing beautiful escaped his eye. If we are to enjoy the beauty about us, there is need of similar *preparation*. What we get out of communion with the beauty of nature or art, depends largely on what we bring to that communion. We must make ourselves sensitive to beauty, or else the charms of form and color and graceful motion and sweet music will be unheeded or unappreciated. It is also true, as Lowell said:

"Thou seest no beauty save thou make it first;
Man, woman, nature, each is but a glass
In which man sees the image of himself."

ALFRED TENNYSON.

Alfred Tennyson, England's greatest modern poet, was a devoted lover of the beautiful from the very beginning of his career. The earliest verses he composed, which were written upon his slate when but a child of seven or eight years of age, had for their subject, "The Flowers in the Garden." As a dreamy boy, he loved to throw himself upon the grass and listen to the bird voices in the adjoining thicket, or to the lowing of the cattle as they stood knee-deep in the glittering waters of the river shallows which lay about his home.

How close an observer he became, even as a lad, is clearly shown in these lines, written as he lay under a tree, listening to the music of the birds:

"The creeping mosses and clambering weeds,
  And the willow branches hoar and dank,
And the wavy swell of the soughing reeds,
  And the wave-worn horns of the echoing bank,
And the silvery marish flowers that throng
The desolate creeks and pools among,
Were flooded over with eddying song."

He became so thoroughly acquainted with the various orders of vegetation with which his native land is clothed, and which mark the progress of the growth and development of plant and flower, that there is scarcely a false note in his music from first to last. His pictures of animal life are drawn in vivid master strokes, and are as notable for their correctness as for their grace. While we cannot speak of him as an astronomer, yet no one can read his verses without admitting that he was a close observer of the starry heavens. We could not rightly give him an equal place with Shelley as a painter of cloud-scenery, yet we know how he loved to lie on his back on the Down of Farringford and watch for hours the swiftly-moving and rapidly-changing panorama of the midday heavens. It was his chiefest joy to dream away his peaceful days among the trees and brooks and flowers. He sometimes spent weeks at a time in the open air wandering for miles in meditative silence along the banks of some sparkling stream, or over the sand and shingle that form the dividing line between the land and sea.

His pictures are photographic in their fidelity, and yet, in them all, the outbursting life and movement of nature is carefully preserved. They cover the widest possible field; dealing with the cloud and sunshine, the storm wind and the zephyr, the roaring of the ocean surge and the murmuring of the running brook, the crashing of the thunder peal and the whisper of the pine-trees. The fields and the hedgerows, the flowers and the grasses, the darkness and the dawn; all are exhibited under every possible shade of variation. His studies of the beautiful are as broad and true to life as any that have ever been written. So sensitive was his soul to these outward impressions of beauty that even those acquired in childhood never entirely passed out of his mind.

[Footnote: On Tennyson, see Dixon's "Tennyson Primer" (New York, 1896); Van Dyke's "Poetry of Tennyson" (New York, 1894); Tainsh's "A Study of Tennyson" (New York, 1893), and Tennyson's Poems.]

VIII.

THE LOYE OF KNOWLEDGE.

MEMORY GEMS.

Knowledge is the eye of the soul.—T. Watson

Common sense is knowledge of common things.—M. C. Peters

It is noble to seek truth, and it is beautiful to find it.
—Sydney Smith

It has cost many a man life or fortune for not knowing what he thought he was sure of.—J. Staples White

The desire of knowledge, like the thirst of riches, increases ever with the acquisition of it.—Sterne

It has been well said that "Nothing is so costly as ignorance. You sow the wrong seed, you plant the wrong field, you build with the wrong timber, you buy the wrong ticket, you take the wrong train, you settle in the wrong locality, or you take the wrong medicine—and no money can make good your mistake."

The knowledge attained by any man appears to be a poor thing to boast of, since there is no condition or situation in which he may be placed without feeling or perceiving that there is something or other which he knows little or nothing about. A man can scarcely open his eyes or turn his head without being able to convince himself of this truth. And yet, without a fair working knowledge of the ordinary affairs of life, every man is, in some respects, as helpless as a child. Indeed there is no kind of knowledge which, in the hands of the diligent and skillful, may not be turned to good account. Honey exudes from all flowers, the bitter not excepted, but the bee knows how to extract it, and, by this knowledge, succeeds in providing for all its needs.

Learning is like a river. At its first rising the river is small and easily viewed, but as it flows onward it increases in breadth and depth, being fed by a thousand smaller streams flowing into it on either side, until at length it pours its mighty torrent into the ocean. So learning, which seems so small to us at the beginning, is ever increasing in its range and scope, until even the greatest minds are unable to comprehend it as a whole.

Sir Isaac Newton felt this when, after his sublime discoveries in science had been accomplished, he said, "I do not know what I may appear to the world; but to myself I seem only like a boy playing upon the seashore, and diverting myself by now and then finding a choice pebble, or a prettier shell than ordinary; while the great ocean of truth lies all undiscovered before me."

Strabo was entitled to be called a profound geographer eighteen hundred years ago, but a geographer who had never heard of America would now be laughed at by boys and girls of ten years of age. What would now be thought of the greatest chemist or geologist of 1776? The truth is that, in every science, mankind is constantly advancing. Every generation has its front and its rear rank; but the rear rank of the later generation stands upon the ground which was occupied by the front rank of its predecessor.

It is important that our knowledge should be as full and complete as we can make it. Partial knowledge nearly always leads us into error. A traveler, as he passed through a large and thick wood, saw a part of a huge oak which appeared misshapen, and almost seemed to spoil the scenery. "If," said he, "I was the owner of this forest, I would cut down that tree." But when he had ascended the hill, and taken a full view of the forest, this same tree appeared the most beautiful part of the landscape. "How erroneously," said he, "I have judged while I saw only a part!" The full view, the harmony and proportion of things, are all necessary to clear up our judgment.

Walter A. Wood, whose keen business ability made him a wealthy man, and sent him to congress as a representative from the great state of New York, is reported to have said, "I would give fifty thousand dollars for a college education." When he came to measure his ability with that of men who had had greater opportunities in an educational line, he realized his loss. Chauncey M. Depew is also reported as having said, "I never saw a self-made man in my life who did not firmly believe that he had been handicapped, no matter how great his success, by deficiency in education, and who was not determined to give his children the advantages of which he felt, not only in business, but in intercourse with his fellow-men, so great a need."

There is a difference between knowledge and wisdom and understanding; but without the first the rest cannot be gained, any more than you can have a harvest of wheat without seed and skill of cultivation. Understanding is the right use of facts; facts make knowledge; knowledge is the root of wisdom. Many men know a great deal, but are not wise or capable; many others know less, but are able to use what they have learned. Wisdom is the ripe fruit of knowledge; knowledge is the beginning of character.

The love of knowledge has been characteristic of most great men. They not only loved knowledge but they were willing to work hard to attain it. As examples of this: Gibbon was in his study every morning, winter and summer, at six o'clock. Milton is said to have stuck to the study of his books with the regularity of a paid bookkeeper. Raphael, the great artist, lived only to the age of thirty-seven, yet so diligent was his pursuit of knowledge, that he carried his art to such a degree of perfection that it became the model for his successors. When a man like one of these wins success, people say "he is a genius." But the real reason for success, was, as you may see, that the love of knowledge led to the effort to obtain it.

Useful knowledge is the knowledge of what is of benefit to ourselves and to others; and that is the most important which is the most useful. It is the belief of those who have spent their lives in the search for it, that knowledge is better than riches, and that its possession brings more comfort to the owner. To be acquainted with the great deeds enacted in past ages; to find out how some nations have grown powerful while others have fallen; or to learn something about the great mysteries of nature, brings with it to the diligent searcher many hours of pleasure. Also the experience of man teaches that the exercise of the mind brings great satisfaction.

Even in seemingly little things the same holds true. There is a fountain in London that is opened by a concealed spring. One day the Bishop of London wanted to drink, but no one could tell him how to open it. At last a little dirty bootblack stepped up and touched the spring and the water gushed out. He knew more than the bishop about that one thing, and so was able to render the great man a real service.

The power of intellectual knowledge, without the power of moral principle, can only tend to evil. It has been said that education would empty our jails; but the greatest criminals, whether of scientific poisoning, or of fraud and forgery, are well educated. It has been asserted lately that "there is a race between scientific detection and prevention, on the one hand, and scientific roguery on the other."

Character is the criterion of knowledge. Not what a man has, but what he is, is the question, after all. The quality of soul is more than the quantity of information. Personal, spiritual substance is the final result. Have that, and your intellectual furnishings and attainments will turn naturally to the loftiest uses. Add obedience to knowledge, and your education will be worth all that it has cost.

ALEXANDER VON HUMBOLDT.

We may further illustrate this topic by a brief glance at the life of Alexander Von Humboldt. His brother, Wilhelm, acquired a distinguished name; but the greater renown fell to the younger, who was born at Berlin, Germany, September 14, 1769,—his full name being Friedrich Heinrich Alexander Von Humboldt. In circumstances of life, his lot was easy; his father had the means to educate him well. No very striking outward event occurred in his youth. Tutors prepared him for college; his own aim was not at once seized. "Until I reached the age of sixteen," he says, "I showed little inclination for scientific pursuits. I was of a restless disposition, and wished to be a soldier."

But another current was flowing in his mind. "From my earliest youth I had an intense desire to travel in those distant lands which have been but rarely visited by Europeans." And again he says: "The study of maps and the perusal of books of travel exercised a secret fascination over me." These early tastes blended at last with a serious purpose, and became "the incentive to scientific labor, or to undertakings of vast import."

To show that Humboldt was not a mere fact-gatherer, we select one incident out of many in his early life. When about twenty-one years of age, he made an extended journey with George Forster over the continent. Forster wrote the following after they had visited the cathedral at Cologne. After describing the glories of the structure he adds: "My attention was arrested by a yet more engrossing object: before me stood a man of lively imagination and refined taste, riveted with admiration to the spot. Oh, it was glorious to see, in his rapt contemplation, the grandeur of the temple repeated as it were by reflection!" In this scene we behold the actual process of knowledge being changed into true learning and ideas; it was always so with Humboldt in his long and varied career.

Humboldt studied hard, held official positions, and matured. His mother died in 1796. To her this son owed much, for the father had died when Alexander was only ten years old, and she watched his education with fidelity. She saw the bent of the "little apothecary,"—as Alexander was called because of his passion for collecting and labeling shells, plants, and insects,—and guided it. Her death set Humboldt free to go afar in travels. In June, 1799, he started on a five years' absence, in which time he climbed Teneriffe and the Cordilleras, explored the Orinoco, visited the United States, and gathered a mass of knowledge which afterward won him lasting fame. Often he was in peril, often baffled, often put to dreary discomforts by savage tribes; but through all ran his unconquerable purpose.

In his scientific work he often took great risks in order to ascertain facts, as all earnest investigators do. In testing a new lamp for miners, he crept into a "crosscut" of the mine, lamp in hand, and continued there so long and persistently that two men rushed in and drew him out by the feet, the gases having overcome him.

We have not space to give details of his splendid career. Humboldt shone with greater light from year to year. Honors were lavished upon him. His works aided science, his life was a constant inspiration. He lived to be ninety years old, dying in 1859,—possessing to the last, a strong memory, and a tireless love of research.

[Footnote: On Humboldt, consult Haym's "Biography of Humboldt" (London, 1856); Bruhn's "Biography of Humboldt" (Leipsic, 1872, translated by the Misses Lassell); Klenke's "Alexander Von Humboldt" (1859); "Humboldt's Correspondence with Goethe" (London, 1876).]

IX.

THE FIRST TRANSITION PERIOD.

MEMORY GEMS.

The child is father of the man.—Wordsworth

Whatever is worth doing at all, is worth doing well.—Chesterfield

No one can cheat you out of ultimate success but yourself.—Emerson

A man cannot live a broad life if he runs only in one groove.
        —J. Staples White

'Tis education forms the common mind,
  Just as the twig is bent the tree's inclined.—Pope

As the child grows into the youth the utmost care should be exercised, both by himself and by his friends, to prevent the dwarfing of his prospects by evil influences arising either from within or from without himself.

The youthful period of man's life is by far the most important. No subsequent training can entirely obliterate the results of early impressions. They may be greatly modified; the character may be changed; but some, and indeed many, of the impressions of youth will cling to the mind forever.

It is in this period that the mind forms the ideas which will govern the will throughout the whole career. Then is the twig bent to the direction in which the tree will grow. The faintest whisperings of counsel are eagerly caught, and the slightest direction instantaneously followed. Then is the seed sown which will bring forth fruit in harvest time.

Bishop Vincent, writing about boyhood, says, "If I were a boy? Ah, if I only were! The very thought of it sets my imagination afire. That 'if' is a key to dreamland. First I would want a thorough discipline, early begun and never relaxed, on the great truth of will force as the secret of character. I would want my teacher to put the weight of responsibility upon me; to make me think that I must furnish the materials and do the work of building my own character; to make me think that I am not a stick, or a stone, or a lump of putty, but a person. That what I am in the long run, is what I am to make myself."

Boys and girls should early form a taste for good reading. In the choice of books, as in the choice of friends, there is but one rule,—choose the best. A witty gentleman, having received an invitation from a wealthy but not very refined lady, on arriving was ushered into her library, where she was seated surrounded by richly-bound books. "You see, Mr. X.," she said, "I never need to be lonely, for here I sit surrounded by my best friends." Without replying, the gentleman approached a shelf and took down a volume which he perceived to be uncut, and smilingly observed, "I am happy to find, madam, that unlike the majority of people, you do not cut your friends."

Macaulay says, "I would rather be a poor man in a garret with plenty of good books to read, than a king who did not love reading."

A boy ten years of age was seen to enter Westminster Abbey shortly before evening prayers. Going straight up the main aisle he stopped at the tomb of Charles Dickens. Then, looking to see that he was not observed, he kneeled before the tombstone, and tenderly placed upon it a bunch of violets. The little fellow hovered affectionately round the spot for a few moments and went away with a happy, contented smile upon his face. Curiosity led a gentleman present to examine the child's offering, and this is what he found written in half-formed letters on an envelope attached to the violets:—

"For it is good to be children sometimes, and never better than at Christmas, when its mighty Founder was a child himself.—Christmas Carol."

The young person that loves books as this little fellow did, will have friends that will unconsciously transform him into a great, noble-hearted man.

It is the thoughts of the boy that shape the future man. Garfield, when asked as a boy, what he was going to do when he grew up, would answer, "First of all I am going to try to be a man. If I become that I shall be fit for anything." To make the most of one's youth is to qualify one's self to become a real man.

Some men, it is true, have been seemingly created by circumstances, and have figured prominently in the world's history. But, as a general rule, the child makes the man; and the foundation of all greatness and usefulness is laid by the impressions of youth. "Alexander the Great would not have been the conqueror of the world had his father not been Philip of Macedon. Hannibal would not have been the scourge of the Romans if Hamilcar had not sworn him to eternal vengeance against his enemies. Napoleon Bonaparte would not have deluged Europe with blood, if he had not been inspired by the genius of war from the pages of Homer." And in our own days, those men whose early impressions were the most favorable have been the most successful, both in their own lives, and in their influence upon the world at large.

But it will not be enough to keep children during the season of youth from the reach of improper associates and influences. The seed of right principles must be diligently sown in their minds. Lessons of purity and conscientiousness must be written deep on the tables of the heart. Parental restraint is outward and visible, but the guiding principles of life are inward and invisible. The day will come when the youth must quit the parental roof, and perhaps entirely bid adieu to the influences of home. If he be then destitute of right principles, if his mind be like a ship without a rudder, he will stand in imminent danger of being swept away by the waves of corruption.

Care should be taken to keep good company or none. No sensible person will willingly keep bad horses or bad dogs. Should he be less particular in selecting his companions? And yet, at this very point, some of life's most cruel blunders are made.

A story is told of two parrots which lived near to each other. The one was accustomed to sing songs, while the other was addicted to swearing. The owner of the latter obtained permission for it to associate with the former, in the hope that its bad habits would be corrected; but the opposite result followed, for both learned to swear alike. This aptly illustrates the usual effect of bad company, and no young man, however strong he may imagine himself to be, can afford to be careless in this matter.

In the forming of your friendships, be less anxious about social standing, and more particular about character. Remember that President Garfield used to say that he never passed a ragged boy in the street without feeling that one day he might owe him a salute, No one knows what possibilities of goodness and greatness are buttoned up under a boy's coat.

On the tomb of Schubert, the great musician, is written, "He gave much, but promised more"; and it is this immeasurable wealth of promise that makes the lives of our boys and girls so full of beauty and of power.

X.

INDUSTRY.

MEMORY GEMS.

Genius is nothing but labor and diligence.—Hogarth.

Know something of everything and everything of something.
—Lord Brougham

The difference between one boy and another lies not so much in talent as in energy.—Dr. Arnold

Work wields the weapons of power, wins the palm of success, and wears the crown of victory.—A. T. Pierson.

A lazy man is of no more use than a dead man, and he takes up more room.—O. S. Harden.

By industry we mean activity that is regular and devoted to the carrying out of some purpose. More definitely, it is activity that is designed to be useful to ourselves or to others. It is thus a *regulated activity* by which our welfare, or that of others, may be furthered.

We are apt to think, or at least to feel, that the necessity of working regularly is a hardship. Because we get tired with our work and look forward with eagerness to the time of rest, we form the opinion that the pleasantest life would be one which should be all rest.

Industry might well be urged as a duty. But we would rather now speak of it chiefly as an aid in accomplishing other duties. Few things are more helpful toward right living than industry, and few more conducive to wrong living than idleness.

No doubt there are on this subject opposing opinions. Some believe, whether they openly confess it or not, that the glory of the highest success is not within the reach of every honest toiler; that it is, like other legacies, the good fortune to which some are heirs, but which others are denied—the inheritance only of those whom nature has well endowed. These are the advocates of genius.

The reader of "Ivanhoe"—that finest romance of Sir Walter Scott—pronounces its author a genius. The fact is, that book is a conspicuous illustration of industry—patient, persevering toil. It has been pointed out that, "for years Scott had made himself familiar with the era of chivalry; plodded over, in imagination, the weary march of the Crusaders; studied the characteristics and contradictions of the Jewish character; searched carefully into the records of the times in which the scenes of his story were laid; and even examined diligently into the strange process whereby the Norman-French and the Anglo-Saxon elements were wrought into a common tongue."

Labor is indeed the price set upon everything which is valuable. Nothing can be accomplished without it. The greatest of men have risen to distinction by unwearied industry and patient application. They may have had inborn genius; their natures may have been quick and active; but they could not avoid the necessity of persevering labor.

Labor is the great schoolmaster of the race. It is the grand drill in life's army, without which we are confused and powerless when called into action. What a teacher industry is! It teaches patience, perseverance, forbearance, and application. It teaches method and system, by compelling us to crowd the most possible into every day and hour. Industry is a perpetual call upon the judgment and the power of quick decision; it makes ready and practical men.

Industry is essential for that usefulness by which each man may fill his place in the world. The lazy, like the wicked, may be made useful. The Spartans used to send a drunken slave through the city that the sight of his folly and degradation might disgust young men with intemperance. He was made useful; he did not make himself useful. From this it will be seen that the necessity of labor is something at which we should rather rejoice than complain, and that habits of industry are the great helpers to virtue, happiness, and usefulness.

Industry is now as important to the woman as to the man. Some years ago, in an art store in Boston, a group of girls stood together gazing intently upon a famous piece of statuary. The silence was broken by the remark, "Just to think that a woman did it." "It makes me proud," said another. The famous statue was that of Zenobia, the product of Harriet Hosmer, whose love of knowledge and devotion to art, gave the world a masterpiece.

Work is difficult in proportion as the end to be attained is high and noble. The highest price is placed upon the greatest worth. If a man would reach the highest success he must pay the price. He must be self-made, or never made.

Our greatest men have not been men of luck and broadcloth, nor of legacy and laziness, but men accustomed to hardship; not afraid of threadbare clothes and honest poverty; men who fought their way to their own loaf.

Sir Joshua Reynolds had the passion for work of the true artist. Until he laid aside his pencil from illness, at the age of sixty-six, he was constantly in his painting-room from ten till four, daily, "laboring" as he himself said, "as hard as a mechanic working for his bread."

Laziness is said to be one of the greatest dangers that besets the youth of this country. Some young men shirk everything that requires effort or labor. Few people entertain the idea that they are of no use in the world; or that they are ruining themselves by their laziness. Yet lazy persons lose the power of enjoyment. Their lives are all holiday, and they have no interval of leisure for relaxation. The lie-a-beds have never done anything in the world. Events sweep past and leave them slumbering and helpless.

Industry is one of the best antidotes to crime. As the old proverb has it, "An idle brain is the devil's workshop," for by doing nothing we learn to do ill. The man who does not work, and thinks himself above it, is to be pitied as well as condemned. Nothing can be worse than active ignorance and indulged luxury. Self-indulgence saps the foundation of morals, destroys the vigor of manhood, and breeds evils that nothing but death can blot out.

No one is very anxious about a young man while he is busy in useful work. But where does he eat his lunch at noon? Where does he go when he leaves his boarding-house at night? What does he do after supper? Where does he spend his Sundays and holidays? The way he uses his spare moments reveals his character. The great majority of youth who go to the bad are ruined after supper. Most of those who climb upward to honor and fame devote their evenings to study or work, or to the society of the wise and good. The right use of these leisure hours, we would cordially recommend to every youth. Each evening is a crisis in the career of a young man.

Rome was a mighty nation while industry led her people, but when her great conquest of wealth and slaves placed her citizens above the necessity of labor, that moment her glory began to fade; vice and corruption induced by idleness, doomed the proud city to an ignominious overthrow.

There can be no doubt that industry has been the backbone of the English character. By it her people have made their island respected all over the habitable globe. By industry our own land has come to be recognized as the workshop of the world.

It is a rule in the imperial family of Germany that every young man shall learn a trade, going through a regular apprenticeship till he is able to do good journeywork. This is required because, in the event of unforeseen changes, it is deemed necessary to a manly independence that the heir apparent, or a prince of the blood, should be conscious of ability of making his own way in the world. This is an honorable custom, worthy of universal imitation. The Jews also wisely held the maxim that every youth, whatever his position in life, should learn some trade.

Franklin says, "He that hath a trade hath an estate." Work, however looked down upon by people who cannot perform it, is an honorable thing; it may not be very profitable, but honorable it always is, and there is nothing to be ashamed of about it. The man who has reason to be ashamed is the one who does nothing, or is always on the lookout for an easy berth with good pay and no work. Let the young man whose conceit greatly exceeds his brains, be ashamed of his cane and kid gloves; but never let a man who works be ashamed of his hard hands. There is an old proverb which says, "Mere gentility sent to market, won't buy a peck of oats."

A keen but well deserved rebuke was once administered to a Southern student at Andover who had bought some wood, and who then went to Professor Stuart to learn whom he could get to saw it. "I am out of a job of that kind," said Mr. Stuart; "I will saw it myself." It is to be hoped that the young man learned the lesson which his teacher thus sought to impress upon his mind.

CORNELIUS VANDERBILT.

"What is the secret of success in business?" asked a friend of Cornelius Vanderbilt. "Secret! there is no secret about it," replied the commodore; "all you have to do is to attend to your business and go ahead."

If you would adopt Vanderbilt's method, know your business, attend to it, and keep down expenses until your fortune is safe from business perils. Note the following incidents in his career: In the year 1806, when about twelve years of age, Cornelius was sent by his father, who was removing the cargo from a vessel stranded near Sandy Hook, with three wagons, six horses, and three men, to carry the cargo across a sandbar to the lighters.

When the work was finished, he started, with but a few dollars in his pocket, to travel a long distance home over the Jersey sands, and at length reached South Amboy. He was anxious to get his teams ferried over to Staten Island, and as the money at his disposal was not sufficient for the purpose, he went to an innkeeper, explained the situation and said, "If you will put us across, I'll leave with you one of my horses in pawn, and if I don't send you back six dollars within forty-eight hours you may keep the horse." "I'll do it," said the innkeeper, as he looked into the bright honest eyes of the boy. The horse was soon redeemed.

In the spring of 1810, he applied to his mother for a loan of one hundred dollars with which to buy a boat, having imbibed a strong liking for the sea. Her answer was, "My son, on the twenty-seventh of this month you will be sixteen years old. If, by that time, you will plow, harrow, and plant with corn the eight acre lot, I will advance you the money." The field was rough and stony, but the work was done in time, and well done. From this small beginning Cornelius Vanderbilt laid the foundation of a colossal fortune. He would often work all night; and, as he was never absent from his post by day, he soon had the best business in New York harbor.

In 1813, when it was expected that New York would be attacked by British ships, all the boatmen, except Cornelius, put in bids to convey provisions to the military posts around New York, naming extremely low rates, as the contractor would be exempted from military duty. "Why don't you send in a bid?" asked his father. "Of what use?" replied young Vanderbilt; "they are offering to do the work at half price. It can't be done at such rates." "Well," said his father, "it can do no harm to try for it." So, to please his father, but with no hope of success, Cornelius made an offer fair to both sides, but did not go to hear the award. When his companions had all returned with long faces, he went to the commissary's office and asked if the contract had been given. "Oh, yes," was the reply; "that business is settled. Cornelius Vanderbilt is the man. What?" he asked, seeing that the youth was apparently thunderstruck, "is it you?" "My name is Cornelius Vanderbilt," said the boatman. "Well," said the commissary, "don't you know why we have given the contract to you? Why, it is because we want this business done, and we know you'll do it."

Here we see how character begets confidence, and how character rests upon industry as the house rests upon its foundation.

[Footnote: Consult Appleton's Cyclopedia of American Biography, Vol. VII., pp. 240, 241; Crofut's "The Vanderbilts and the Story of their Fortune" (1886); also article in Munsey's Magazine, Vol. VI., p. 34.]

XI.

AMBITION.

MEMORY GEMS.

Hope without an object cannot live.—Coleridge

Have an aim in life, or your energies will all be wasted.
—M. C. Peters

Every one should take the helm of his own life, and steer instead of
drifting.—C. C. Everett

Ambition is to life just what steam is to the locomotive.
—J. C. Jaynes

No toil, no hardships can restrain ambitious men inur'd to pain.—Horace

Ambition is one of the great forces of human life. We may describe it as a strong, fixed desire in the heart to get honor, or to attain the best things. It is a kind of hunger or thirst for success that makes men dare danger and trial to satisfy it. A man is of little use in the world unless he have ambition to set him in motion. Small talent with great ambition often does far more than genius without it.

The severest censure that can be passed upon a man is that of the poet, "Everything by turns and nothing long." The words contain a sad revelation of wasted opportunities, wasted powers, wasted life. These words apply, with a painful degree of exactness, to the career of Lord Brougham. Few men have been more richly endowed by nature. Few men have exhibited a greater plasticity of intellect, a greater affluence of mental resources. He was a fine orator, a clear thinker, a ready writer. It is seldom that a man who sways immense audiences by the power of his eloquence attains also to a high position in the ranks of literature. Yet Brougham did this; while, as a lawyer, he gained the most splendid prize of his profession, the Lord Chancellorship of England; and as a scientific investigator, merited and received the applause of scientific men.

All this may seem to indicate success; and, to a certain extent, Brougham was successful. Nevertheless, having been everything by turns and nothing long—having given up to many pursuits the powers which should have been reserved for one or two—he was on the whole, a failure. Not only did he fail to make any permanent mark on the history or literature of his country, but he even outlived his own fame. He was almost forgotten before he died. He frittered away his genius on too many objects.

It has long been a question of debate whether circumstances make men, or men control circumstances. There are those who believe that men are governed by their environments; that their surroundings determine their lives.

The other school of philosophers boldly assert the opposite view. Men may control their surroundings. They are not the sport of the winds of circumstance. Carlyle, who is a member of this school, does not hesitate, in one of his essays, to say that "there have been great crises in the world's history when great men were needed, but they did not appear."

This much is certain, we have many instances in which people have risen above their surroundings. Warren Hastings's case is one in point. Macaulay tells the story with his accustomed brilliancy and attractiveness. When Hastings was a mere child, the ancestral estate, through some mismanagement, passed out of the hands of the family. Warren would often go—for the family remained in the neighborhood—and gaze through the bars upon what had once been his home. He registered a mental vow to regain that estate. That became the ambition of his life; the one great purpose to which he devoted all his energies. Many years passed; Hastings went to other climes; but there was ever with him the determination to get that estate; and he succeeded.

After all, would it not appear that the true theory is .that of a golden mean between these two extremes? Circumstances sometimes control men or, at any rate, some kind of men; men, especially men of strong will power sometimes control their environments. Circumstances give men an opportunity to display their powers. The fuller study of this subject clearly shows the need of some principles of morality that are not dependent upon any chance companionship, and that may belong to the man himself, and not merely to his surroundings.

An ambition to get on in the world, the steady struggle to get up, to reach higher, is a constant source of education in foresight, in prudence, in economy, in industry and courage; in fact is the great developer of many of the strongest and noblest qualities of character.

The men at the summit fought their way up from the bottom. "John Jacob Astor sold apples on the streets of New York; A. T. Stewart swept out his own store; Cornelius Vanderbilt laid the foundation of his vast fortune with a hundred dollars given him by his mother; Lincoln was a rail splitter; Grant was a tanner; and Garfield was a towboy on a canal."

By hard work and unconquerable perseverance you can rise above the low places of poverty. True, you may never shine in the galaxy of the great ones of this earth, but you may fill your lives and homes with blessings, and make the world wiser and better for your having lived in it. Cash cannot take the place of character. It is far better to be a man, than merely to be a millionaire.

A man who heard Lincoln speak in Norwich, Connecticut, some time before he was nominated for the presidency, was greatly impressed by the closely-knit logic of the speech. Meeting him next day on a train, he asked him how he acquired his wonderful logical powers and such acuteness in analysis. Lincoln replied: "It was my terrible discouragement which did that for me. When I was a young man I went into an office to study law. I saw that a lawyer's business is largely to prove things. I said to myself, 'Lincoln, when is a thing proved?' That was a poser. What constitutes proof? Not evidence; that was not the point. There may be evidence enough, but wherein consists the proof? I groaned over the question, and finally said to myself, 'Ah! Lincoln, you can't tell.' Then I thought, 'What use is it for me to be in a law office if I can't tell when a thing is proved?' So I gave it up and went back home.

"Soon after I returned to the old log cabin, I fell in with a copy of Euclid. I had not the slightest notion what Euclid was, and I thought I would find out. I therefore began, at the beginning, and before spring I had gone through that old Euclid's geometry, and could demonstrate every proposition like a book. Then in the spring, when I had got through with it, I said to myself one day, 'Ah, do you know now when a thing is proved?' And I answered, 'Yes, sir, I do.' 'Then you may go back to the law shop;' and I went."

We may be rightly ambitious in various ways. It is right to be ambitious for *fame and honor*. The love of praise is not bad in itself, but it is a very dangerous motive. Why? Because in order to be popular, one may be tempted to be insincere. Never let the world's applause drown the voice of conscience.

It is right to be ambitious to excel in whatever you do. Slighted work and half-done tasks are sins. "I am as good as they are"; "I do my work as well as they"; are cowardly maxims. Not what others have done, but perfection, is the only true aim, whether it be in the ball-field or in the graver tasks of life.

Many people think that ambition is an evil weed, and ought to be pulled up by the roots. Shakespeare makes Wolsey say,—

"I charge thee, fling away ambition
  By that sin fell the angels."

But the great cardinal had abused ambition, and had changed it into a vice. Ambition is a noble quality in itself, but like any other virtue it may be carried to excess, and thus become an evil. Like fire or water, it must be controlled to be safe and useful. Napoleon, while commanding armies, could not command his own ambition; and so he was caged up like a wild beast at St. Helena. A millionaire may be so ambitious for gain as purposely to wreck the fortunes of others. A politician may sell his manhood to gratify his desire for office. Boys and girls may become so ambitious to win their games, or to get the prizes at school, that they are willing to cheat, or take some mean advantage; and then ambition becomes to them not a blessing but a curse.

We ought now and then to stop and test our ambition, just as the engineer tries the steam in the boiler; if we do not, it may in some unexpected moment wreck our lives. There are two ways of finding out whether our ambition is too strong for safety. First, if we discover that ambition is hurting our own character, there is danger. Second, if we find ambition blinding us to the rights of others, it is time to stop. These are the two tests; and so long as your ambition is harming neither your own life nor the lives of others, it is good and wholesome, and will add value and brightness to your life.

GENERAL HAVELOCK.

Henry Havelock, commonly known as "The Hero of Lucknow," was born in England, 1795, just about the time when Napoleon was beginning his brilliant career, and all Europe was a battlefield. As a boy he was rather serious and thoughtful, so that his school fellows used to call him "Old Phlos," a nickname for Old Philosopher. And yet he loved boyish sports, and never was behind any of his companions in courage and daring.

He was not the first scholar in his class, but he was a great reader and took intense delight in stories of war and descriptions of battles. Napoleon was his hero, and he watched all his movements with breathless interest; and soon began to dream of being a soldier, too. Thus was born in the boy's heart that ambition which afterward lifted the man into honor and fame.

At the age of sixteen Havelock began to study law, but he soon tired of it, and three years later obtained an appointment in the army. He now gave himself, with all the love and enthusiasm of his nature, to his chosen profession. He was to be a soldier; and he decided that he would be a thorough one, and would understand the art of war completely. He studied very hard, and it is said that it was his habit to draw with a stick upon the ground the plan of some historic battlefield, then, in imagination fight the battle over again, so that he might clearly see what made the one side lose and the other win.

After eight years of service in England, he was ordered to go to India. There he became a soldier in earnest. It would take too long to tell of the battles he was in, and of the terrible campaigns through which he served. It is enough to say that he always followed where duty led, and always seemed to know just what to do amid the confusion of the battlefield. It was the dream of his life to become a general, but he was doomed, year after year, to stand still and see untried, beardless men promoted above his head. This certainly was hard to bear, but he never lost heart, never sulked, never neglected any opportunity to serve his government. His ambition was to do his best; and this he did, whether the world saw and applauded or not.

Until he reached the age of sixty-two, he was scarcely known outside of India; but then came the occasion that made him famous. All India was in mutiny. The native soldiers, mad with power, were murdering the English in every city. Far up in the interior, at Lucknow, was a garrison of English soldiers, women, and children, hemmed in by thousands of these bloodthirsty Sepoys. To surrender meant a horrible death. To hold the fort meant starvation at last, unless rescue should speedily come.

Although, when the news reached him, he was hundreds of miles away, Havelock undertook to save that little garrison. It seemed an impossible task, and yet with a few hundred brave soldiers, in a country swarming with the enemy, through swamps, over swollen rivers, he fought his way to the gates at Lucknow. And then, beneath a hailstorm of bullets from every house-top, he marched up the narrow street, and never paused until he stood within the fortress walls, and heard the shout of welcome from the lips of the starving men and women. It was a wonderful march, and put him among the great soldiers of history; but it was the direct result of that powerful ambition which had influenced his entire career.

The world rang with applause of his heroism; but praise came too late; for while the queen was making him a baronet, and Parliament was voting him a princely pension, he was dying of a fever within the very city he had so bravely stormed. But his life-work was fully completed, and his name shines brightly among those of the great military heroes of his native land.

[Footnote: See Marshman's "Life of Havelock" (1860); Headley's "Life of Havelock" (1864); Brock's "Life of General Sir Henry Havelock" (1854); Molesworth's "History of England," Vol. III., Chap, ii., and Mitchell's "History of India" (London, 1895).]

XII.

CONCENTRATION.

MEMORY GEMS.

Success grows out of struggles to overcome difficulties.—Smiles

He who follows two hares is sure to catch neither.—Franklin

The important thing in life is to have a great aim and the determination to attain it.—Goethe

A healthy definite purpose is a remedy for a thousand ills.
—O. S. Marden

The evidence of superior genius is the power of intellectual
  concentration.—B. R. Hayden

Concentration begins with the habit of attention. The highest success in
learning depends on the power of the learner to command and hold his own
attention,—on his ability to concentrate his thought on the subject before
him. By the words "habit of attention," we do not mean here the outward,
respectful attitude of a docile pupil who listens when his teacher speaks, but
something much rarer, much more important, and far more difficult of
attainment. We mean that power of the mind by which a person is able to
give an intelligent account of what is said, whether in conversation, in lecture,
or in sermon; which enables him to grasp at one reading the important points
of a problem or a paragraph; and which makes it possible for a student or a
reader to so concentrate his attention on what he is doing as to be entirely
oblivious, so long as it does not concern him, of what is going on around
him.

This is the age of concentration or specialization of energy. The problem of
the day is to get ten-horse power out of an engine that shall occupy the space
of a one-horse power engine, and no more. Just so society demands a ten-
man power out of one individual. It crowns the man who knows one thing
supremely, and can do it better than anybody else, even if it be only the art
of raising turnips. If he raises the best turnips by reason of concentrating all
his energy to that end, he is a benefactor to the race, and is recognized as
such. The giants of the race have been men of concentration, who have
struck all their blows in one place until they have accomplished their purpose.
The successful men of today are men of one overmastering idea, one
unwavering aim, men of single and intense purpose. "Scatteration" is the
curse of American business life. Too many are like Douglas Jerrold's friend,
who could converse in twenty-four languages, but had no ideas to express in
any one of them.

"The weakest living creature," says Carlyle, "by concentrating his powers on
a single object, can accomplish something; whereas the strongest, by
dispersing his over many, may fail to accomplish anything. The drop, by
continually falling, bores its passage through the hardest rock. The hasty
torrent rushes over it with hideous uproar and leaves no trace behind."

It is interesting to read how, with an immense procession passing up
Broadway, the streets lined with people, and the bands playing their loudest,
Horace Greeley would sit upon the steps of the Astor House, use the top of
his hat for a desk, and write an editorial for the New York *Tribune* which
would be quoted all over the country; and there are many incidents in his
career which go to show that his wonderful power of concentration was one
of the great secrets of his success.

Men who have the right kind of material in them will assert their personality, and rise in spite of a thousand adverse circumstances. You cannot keep them down. Every obstacle seems only to add their ability to get on. The youth Opie earned his bread by sawing wood, but he reached a professorship in the Royal Academy. When but ten years old he showed the material he was made of by a beautiful drawing on a shingle. Antonio Canova was a son of a day laborer; Thorwaldsen's parents were poor; but, like hundreds of others, these men did with their might what their hands found to do, and ennobled their work. They rose by being greater than their calling.

It is fashionable to ridicule the man of one idea; but the men who have changed the face of the world have been men of a single aim. No man can make his mark on this age of specialities who is not a man of one idea, one supreme aim, one master passion. The man who would make himself felt on this bustling planet, must play all his guns on one point. A wavering aim, a faltering purpose, will have no place in the twentieth century. "Mental shiftlessness" is the cause of many a failure. The world is full of unsuccessful men who spend their lives letting empty buckets down into empty wells.

As opposed to men of the latter class, what a sublime picture of determination and patience was that of Charles Goodyear, of New Haven, buried in poverty and struggling with hardships for eleven long years, to make India rubber of practical use! See him in prison for debt; pawning his clothes and his wife's jewelry to get a little money to buy food for his children, who were obliged to gather sticks in the field for fire. Observe the sublime courage and devotion to his idea, when he had no money to bury a dead child, and when his other five were near starvation; when his neighbors were harshly criticising him for his neglect of his family, and calling him insane. But, behold his vulcanized rubber; the result of that heroic struggle, applied to thousands of uses by over sixty thousand employees.

A German knight undertook to make an immense Aeolian harp by stretching wires from tower to tower of his castle. When he finished the harp it was silent; but when the breezes began to blow he heard faint strains like the murmuring of distant music. At last a tempest arose and swept with fury over his castle, and then rich and grand music came from the wires. Ordinary experiences do not seem to touch some lives, to bring out their higher manhood; but when patience and firmness bring forth their fruit it is always of the very finest quality.

It is good to know that great people have done great things through concentration; but it is better still to know that concentration belongs to the everyday life of the everyday boy and girl. Only they must not be selfish about it. Understand the work in hand before it is begun. Don't think of anything else while doing it; and don't dream when learning a lesson. Do one thing at a time and do it quickly and thoroughly. "I go at what I am about," said Charles Kingsley, "as if there was nothing else in the world for the time being." That's the secret of the success of all hard-working men.

S. T. Coleridge possessed marvelous powers of mind, but he had no definite purpose; he lived in an atmosphere of mental dissipation, which consumed his energy and exhausted his stamina, and his life was in many respects a miserable failure. He lived in dreams and died in reverie. He was continually forming plans and resolutions, but to the day of his death they remained resolutions and plans. He was always just going to do something, but never did it. "Coleridge is dead," wrote Charles Lamb to a friend, "and is said to have left behind him above forty thousand treatises on metaphysics and divinity—not one of them complete!"

Commodore MacDonough, on Lake Champlain, concentrated the fire of all his vessels upon the "big ship" of Downie, regardless of the fact that the other British ships were all hurling cannon balls at his little fleet. The guns of the big ship were silenced, and then the others were taken care of easily.

By exercising this art of concentration in a higher degree than did his brother generals, Grant was able to bring the Civil War to a speedy termination. This trait was strongly marked in the character of Washington. The same is true in regard to General Armstrong and the Hampton Institute. That stands as a living monument to his power of concentration. He had a great purpose: the education of the Negro and Indian races; and from the close of the Civil War to the day of his death he labored steadily at that one undertaking, and now the whole country is proud of the outcome of his toil.

People who have concentration never make excuses. They get more done than others, and have a better time doing it. Excuses are signs of shiftlessness. They do not answer in play any better than in lessons or business. Who ever heard of excuses in football-playing? When we go into all our duties with the same earnestness and devotion, we shall find ourselves rapidly rising into one of those foremost places which most of us so greatly desire.

DAVID LIVINGSTONE.

Few men in this century have followed a single purpose through their entire lives with greater devotion than the famous missionary and explorer, David Livingstone.

He was born in Scotland, March 19, 1813, of poor parents. He loved books as a boy, studied hard to know about rocks and plants, worked in a cotton mill and earned money to go to a medical school. He was honest, helped his mother, and read all the books he could. "My reading in the factory," he said, "was carried on by placing the book on a portion of the spinning-jenny, so that I could catch sentence after sentence as I passed at my work. I thus kept up a pretty constant study, undisturbed by the roar of machinery."

Very early Livingstone began to think about being a missionary. He read about travels in Africa, about the work of Henry Martyn, and about the Moravian missions. He heard about China and the need of medical missionaries there; and he says that "from this time my efforts were constantly devoted toward this object without any fluctuation."

Livingstone wanted to go to China; but he met Dr. Moffat, who was then home from Africa, and was persuaded to change his plans. Early in 1841 he reached Algoa Bay, at the south end of Africa. Then he went to Dr. Moffat's mission station at Kuruman; but here he found the missionaries did not work well together, that there were more men than work, so he pushed on into regions where no one had been before. "I really am ambitious," he wrote, "to preach beyond other men's lines. I am determined to go on, and do all I can, while able, for the poor, degraded people in the North."

This feeling sent him into the great wilderness to find what opportunities it afforded. In 1852 he started on his first great journey, made more discoveries, and crossed Africa from east to west, and then back again to the east coast. It was hard work; many were the difficulties; and his life was often in peril. Yet he saw Africa as no one before had seen it; and when he returned to England in 1857 he found himself famous, honored on every hand, and everybody ready to help on his great and noble work.

In 1859 he returned to Africa with men and money to explore further, and to see what could be done for the good of the country. He explored the Zambezi river, on the east coast; and became familiar with that side of Africa,—its people, rivers, lakes, and mountains. He returned home in 1864, but went back the next year to seek out the source of the Nile. In 1865 he started on his longest and last journey, going this time to the northwest. This was the hardest and most perilous of all his journeys; for he was often sick, his men were not faithful, the country was in a state of war, his money gave out; and he was in a very bad condition when Henry M. Stanley found him in 1871.

Stanley furnished him with money and men, and he started again for the great interior region to discover the source of the Nile, and then to return home and die. He was now sixty years old, his health had given way, but he persisted in the effort to finish his work. He grew weaker from month to month, but would not turn back. Finally, on May 1, 1873, his men found him on his knees in his tent, dead; but the results of his patient and persevering efforts will never die.

[Footnote: Consult Livingstone's "Last Journals" (1874); Blaikie's "Life of Livingstone;" and Stanley's "How I found Livingstone" (1873).]

XIII.

SELF-CONTROL.

MEMORY GEMS.

Self-mastery is the essence of heroism.—Emerson

He who reigns within himself is more than a king.—Milton

I have only one counsel for you—Be master!—Napoleon

Self-control is essential to happiness and usefulness.—E. A. Horton

He is a fool who cannot be angry; but he is a wise man who will not.—Old Proverb

Some one has said "Self-control is only courage under another form"; but we think it is far more than that. It is the master of all the virtues, courage included. If it is not so, how can it so control them as to develop a pure and noble character? The self-control which we commend has its root in true self-respect. The wayward, drifting youth or man cannot respect himself. He knows that there is no decision of character in drifting with the current, no enterprise, spirit, or determination. He must look the world squarely in the face, and say, "I am a man," or he cannot respect himself; and he must stem the current and row up stream to command his destiny.

Self-control is at the root of all the virtues. Let a man yield to his impulses and passions, and from that moment he gives up his moral freedom. "Teach self-denial and make its practice pleasurable," says Walter Scott, "and you create for the world a destiny more sublime than ever issued from the brain of the wildest dreamer."

This may seem to be a very strong statement, but it is fully sustained by the experience of great men like Dr. Cuyler, who said, not long ago, "I have been watching the careers of young men by the thousand in this busy city of New York for over thirty years, and I find that the chief difference between the successful and the unsuccessful lies in the single element of 'staying-power.'"

Think of a man just starting out in life to conquer the world being at the mercy of his own appetites and passions! He cannot stand up and look the world in the face when he is the slave of what should be his own servants. He cannot lead who is led. There is nothing which gives certainty and direction to the life of a man who is not his own master. If he has mastered all but one appetite, passion, or weakness, he isstill a slave; it is the weakest point that measures the strength of character.

It was the self-discipline of a man who had never looked upon war until he was forty, that enabled Oliver Cromwell to create an army which never fought without victory, yet which retired into the ranks of industry as soon as the government was established, each soldier being distinguished from his neighbors only by his superior diligence, sobriety, and regularity in the pursuits of peace.

Many of the greatest characters in history illustrate this trait. Take, as a single instance, the case of the Duke of Wellington, whose career was marked by a persistent watchfulness over his irritable and explosive nature. How well he conquered himself, let the story of his deeds tell. The field of his great victory, which was Napoleon's overthrow, could not have been won but for this power of subduing himself.

In ordinary life the application is the same. He who would lead must first command himself. The time of test is when everybody is excited or angry or dismayed; then the well-balanced mind comes to the front. To say, "No" in the face of glowing temptation is a part of this power.

A very striking illustration is recorded in the life of Horace Greeley. Offended by a pungent article, a gentleman called at the *Tribune* office and inquired for the editor. He was shown into a little seven-by-nine sanctum, where Greeley sat, with his head close down to his paper, scribbling away at a rapid rate. The angry man began by asking if this was Mr. Greeley. "Yes, sir; what do you want?" said the editor, quickly, without once looking up from his paper. The irate visitor then began using his tongue, with no deference to the rules of propriety, good breeding, or reason. Meantime Mr. Greeley continued to write. Page after page was dashed off in the most impetuous style, with no change of features, and without paying the slightest attention to the visitor. Finally, after about twenty minutes of the most impassioned scolding ever poured out in an editor's office, the angry man became disgusted, and abruptly turned to walk out of the room. Then, for the first time, Mr. Greeley looked up, rose from his chair, and slapping the gentleman familiarly on his shoulder, in a pleasant tone of voice said: "Don't go, friend; sit down, sit down, and free your mind; it will do you good, you will feel better for it. Besides, it helps me to think what I am to write about. Don't go."

There is a very special demand for the cultivation of this trait and the kindred grace of patience at the present time. "Can't wait" is characteristic of the century, and is written on everything; on commerce, on schools, on societies, on churches. Can't wait for high school seminary or college. The boy can't wait to become a youth, nor the youth a man. Young men rush into business with no great reserve of education or drill; of course they do poor, feverish work, and break down in middle life, and may die of old age at forty, if not before. Everybody is in a hurry; and to be able, amid this universal rush, to hold one's self in check, and to stick to a single object until it is fully accomplished, will carry us a long way toward success.

Endurance is a much better test of character than any one act of heroism, however noble. It was many years of drudgery, and reading a thousand volumes, that enabled George Eliot to get fifty thousand dollars for "Daniel Deronda."

Edison in describing his repeated efforts to make the phonograph reproduce a sibilant sound, says, "From eighteen to twenty hours a day for the last seven months I have worked on this single word 'specia.' I said into the phonograph 'specia, specia, specia;' but the instrument responded 'pecia, pecia, pecia.' It was enough to drive one mad. But I held firm, and I have succeeded."

Years of patient apprenticeship make a man a good mechanic. It takes longer to form the artisan. The trained intellect requires a longer period still. Henry Ward Beecher sent a half-dozen articles to the publishers of a religious paper to pay for his subscription, but they were "respectfully declined." One of the leading magazines ridiculed Tennyson's first poems, and consigned the young poet to oblivion. Only one of Ralph Waldo Emerson's books had a remunerative sale. Washington Irving was nearly seventy years old before the income from his books paid the expenses of his household. Who does not see that if these men had lost their grip upon themselves, the world would have been deprived of many of its rarest literary treasures?

A great many rules have been given for securing and increasing this trait. A large number rest on mere policy, and are good only for the surface; they do not go to the center. Others are too radical, and tear up the roots, leaving one without energy or ambition. The aim should be to keep the native force unabated, but to give it wiser guidance.

A fair amount of self-examination is good. Self-knowledge is a preface to self-control. The wise commander knows the weak and strong points of his fort. Too much self-inspection leads to morbidness; too little, conducts to careless, hasty action. The average American does not know himself well enough; he proceeds with a boastful confidence, and is always in the right, so he thinks. If we are conscious of a failing we naturally strive against it.

There are two chief aims which, if held in view, will surely strengthen our self-control; one is attention to conscience, the other is a spirit of good-will. The lawless nature, not intending to live according to right, is always breaking over proper restraints,—is suspicious and quarrelsome. And he who has not the disposition to love his fellow-men, grows more and more petulant, disagreeable, and unfair.

You must also learn to guard your weak point. For example: Have you a hot, passionate temper? If so, a moment's outbreak, like a rat-hole in a dam, may flood all the work of years. One angry word sometimes raises a storm that time itself cannot allay. A single angry word has lost many a friend. The man who would succeed in any great undertaking must hold all his faculties under perfect control; they must be disciplined and drilled, until they quickly and cheerfully obey the will.

GEORGE WASHINGTON.

For the special illustration of this lesson we select a couple of incidents from the life of George Washington.

Washington had great power of wrath, inheriting the high, hasty temper of his mother. Tobias Lear, his intimate friend and private secretary, says that in the winter of 1791, an officer brought a letter telling of General St. Clair's disastrous defeat by the Indians. It must be delivered to the President himself. He left his family and guests at table, glanced over the contents, and, when he rejoined them, seemed as calm as usual. But afterward, when he and Lear were alone, walked the room, silent a while, and then he broke out in great agitation, "It is all over. St. Clair is defeated, routed; the officers nearly all killed, the men by wholesale; the disaster complete; too shocking to think of, and a surprise into the bargain!" He walked about, much agitated, and his wrath became terrible. "Yes!" he burst forth, "here on this very spot, I took leave of him. I wished him success and honor. 'You have your instructions,' I said, 'from the Secretary of War. I had myself a strict eye to them, and will add but one word, BEWARE OF A SURPRISE! You know how the Indians fight!'

"He went off with this, as my last solemn warning, thrown into his ears; and yet, to suffer that army to be cut to pieces, hacked, butchered, tomahawked, by a surprise,—the very thing I guarded him against! O God! O God! he is worse than a murderer! How can he answer for it to his country? The blood of the slain is upon him; the curse of widows and orphans; the curse of Heaven!"

His emotions were awful. After a while he cooled a little, and sat down, and said: "This must not go beyond this room. General St. Clair shall have justice. I looked through the despatches, saw the whole disaster, but not all the particulars. I will receive him without displeasure; I will hear him without prejudice. He shall have full justice!"

The second incident is told as follows: In 1775, at Cambridge, the army was destitute of powder. Washington sent Colonel Glover to Marblehead for a supply of that article, which was said to be there. At night the colonel returned, found Washington in front of his headquarters, pacing up and down. Glover saluted. The general, without returning his salute, asked, roughly: "Have you got the powder?" "No, sir." Washington broke out at first with terrible severity of speech, and then said: "Why did you come back, sir, without it?" "Sir, there is not a kernel of powder in Marblehead."

Washington walked up and down a minute or two, in great agitation, and then said: "Colonel Glover, here is my hand, if you will take it and forgive me. The greatness of our danger made me forget what is due to you and to myself."

Such victories as these show self-control at its very best; and they ought to make us all see its value and importance.

[Footnote: See Seeley's "Story of Washington" (1893), and the excellent article in Appleton's Cyclopedia of American Biography, Vol. VI., pp. 376-382.]

XIV.

PEKSEVERANCE.

MEMORY GEMS.

Every noble work is at first impossible.—Carlyle

Victory belongs to the most persevering.—Napoleon

Our greatest glory is, not in never falling, but in rising every time we fall.—Goldsmith

Success in most things depends on knowing how long it takes to succeed.
—Montesquieu

Perseverance is failing nineteen times and succeeding the twentieth.
—Dr J. Anderson

Perseverance depends on three things,—purpose, will, enthusiasm. He who has a purpose is always concentrating his forces. By the will, constantly educated, the hope and plan are prevented from evaporating into dreams, and a little gain is all the time being added. Enthusiasm keeps the interest up, and makes the obstacles seem small. Young people often call perseverance plodding, and look with impatience on careful, steady efforts of any kind. It is plodding in a certain sense, but by it the mountain is scaled; whereas the impetuous nature soon tires, or is injured, and the climb is over, half-finished. The founders of New England did not believe in "chances." They did believe in work. The young man who thinks to get on by mere smartness and by idling, meets failure at last.

But there is a higher outlook. Life is in a sense a battle; certainly there is an unending struggle within ourselves to make the better part rule the worse. Perseverance is the master impulse of the firmest souls, and holds the key to those treasure-houses of knowledge from which the world has drawn its wealth both of wisdom and of moral worth.

Great men never wait for opportunities; they make them. Nor do they wait for facilities or favoring circumstances; they seize upon whatever is at hand, work out their problem, and master the situation. A young man determined and willing, will find a way or make one. Great men have found no royal road to their triumph. It is always the old route, by way of industry and perseverance.

Bunyan wrote his "Pilgrim's Progress" on the untwisted papers used to cork the bottles of milk brought for his meals. Gifford wrote his first copy of a mathematical work, when a cobbler's apprentice, on small scraps of leather; and Rittenhouse, the astronomer, first calculated eclipses on his plow handle.

"Circumstances," says Milton, "have rarely favored famous men. They have fought their way to triumph through all sorts of opposing obstacles. The greatest thing a man can do in this world is to make the most possible out of the stuff that has been given to him. This is success, and there is no other."

Paris was in the hands of a mob; the authorities were panic-stricken, for they did not dare to trust their underlings. In came a man who said, "I know a young officer who has the courage and ability to quell this mob." "Send for him; send for him," said they. Napoleon was sent for, came, subjugated the mob, subjugated the authorities, ruled France, then conquered Europe.

One of the first lessons of life is to learn how to get victory out of defeat. It takes courage and stamina, when mortified and embarrassed by humiliating disaster, to seek in the wreck or ruins the elements of future conquest. Yet this measures the difference between those who succeed and those who fail. You cannot measure a man by his failures. You must know what use he makes of them.

Always watch with great interest a young man's first failure. It is the index of his life, the measure of his success-power. The mere fact of his failure has interest; but how did he take his defeat? What did he do next? Was he discouraged? Did he slink out of sight? Did he conclude that he had made a mistake in his calling, and dabble in something else? Or was he up and at it again with a determination that knows no defeat?

There is something grand and inspiring in a young man who fails squarely after doing his level best, and then enters the contest again and again with undaunted courage and redoubled energy. Have no fears for the youth who is not disheartened at failure.

Raleigh failed, but he left a name ever to be linked with brave effort and noble character. Kossuth did not succeed, but his lofty career, his burning words, and his ideal fidelity will move men for good as long as time shall last. O'Connell did not win his cause, but he did achieve enduring fame as an orator, patriot, and apostle of liberty.

President Lincoln was asked, "How does Grant impress you as a leading general?" "The greatest thing about him is his persistency of purpose," he replied. "He is not easily excited, and he has the grip of a bulldog. When he once gets his teeth in nothing can shake him off."

Chauncey Jerome's education was limited to three months in the district school each year until he was ten, when his father took him into his blacksmith shop at Plymouth, Connecticut, to make nails. Money was a scarce article with young Chauncey. His father died when he was eleven, and his mother was forced to send him out to earn a living on a farm. At fourteen he was apprenticed for seven years to a carpenter, who gave him only board and clothes. One day he heard people talking of Eli Terry, of Plymouth, who had undertaken to make two hundred clocks in one lot. "He'll never live long enough to finish them," said one. "If he should," said another, "he could not possibly sell so many. The very idea is ridiculous."

Chauncey pondered long over this rumor, for it had long been his dream to become a great clock-maker. He tried his hand at the first opportunity, and soon learned to make a wooden clock. When he got an order to make twelve at twelve dollars apiece he thought his fortune was made.

One night he happened to think that a cheap clock could be made of brass as well as of wood, and would not shrink, swell, or warp appreciably in any climate. He acted on the idea, and became the first great manufacturer of brass clocks. He made millions at the rate of six hundred a day, exporting them to all parts of the globe.

A constant struggle, a ceaseless battle to bring success from hard surroundings, is the price of all great achievements. The man who has not fought his way upward, and does not bear the scar of desperate conflict, does not know the highest meaning of success.

Columbus was dismissed as a fool from court after court, but he pushed his suit against an unbelieving and ridiculing world. Rebuffed by kings, scorned by queens, he did not swerve a hair's breadth from the overmastering purpose which dominated his soul. The words "New World" were graven upon his heart; and reputation, ease, pleasure, position, life itself, if need be, must be sacrificed. Neither threats, ridicule, storms, leaky vessels, nor mutiny of sailors, could shake his mighty purpose.

Lucky for the boy who can say, "In the bright lexicon of youth there is no such word as *fail*." We do not care for the men who change with every wind! Give us men like mountains, who change the winds. You cannot at one dash rise into eminence. You must hammer it out by steady and rugged blows.

A man can get what he wants if he pays the price—persistent, plodding perseverance. Never doubt the result; victory will be yours. There may be ways to fortune shorter than the old, dusty highway; but the staunch men in the community all go on this road. If you want to do anything, don't stand back waiting for a better chance to arise, but rush in and seize it; and then cling to it with all the power you possess until you have made it serve the purpose for which you desired it, or yield the good which you believe it to contain.

The lack of perseverance is the cause of many a failure. We do not stand by our plans faithfully. Fashion, or criticism, or temporary weariness, or fickleness of taste, leads us off; and we have to begin our work all over. Look at the history of every noted invention; read the lives of musicians who were born with genius, but wrought out triumph by perseverance; and you will find abundant proof that without perseverance nothing valuable can be accomplished.

GEORGE STEPHENSON.

George Stephenson's struggle for the adoption of his locomotive is another noteworthy case in point. People said "he is crazy"; "his roaring steam engine will set the houses on fire with its sparks"; "the smoke will pollute the air"; "the carriage makers and coachmen will starve for want of work." So intense was the opposition, that for three whole days the matter was debated in the House of Commons; and on that occasion a government inspector said that if a locomotive ever went ten miles an hour, he would undertake to eat a stewed engine for breakfast. "What can be more palpably absurd and ridiculous than the prospect held out of locomotives traveling twice as fast as horses?" asked a writer in the English *Quarterly Review* for March, 1825. "We trust that Parliament will, in all the railways it may grant, *limit the speed to eight or nine miles an hour*, which we entirely agree, with Mr. Sylvester, is as great as can be ventured upon."

This article referred to Stephenson's proposition to use his newly invented locomotive instead of horses on the Liverpool and Manchester Railway, then in process of construction. The company referred the matter to two leading English engineers, who reported that steam would be desirable only when used in stationary engines one and a half miles apart, drawing the cars by means of ropes and pulleys.

But Stephenson persuaded them to test his idea by offering a prize of about twenty-five hundred dollars for the best locomotive produced at a trial to take place October 6, 1829. On the eventful day, long waited for, thousands of spectators assembled to watch the competition of four engines, the "Novelty," the "Rocket," the "Perseverance," and the "Sanspareil." The "Perseverance" could make but six miles an hour, and so was ruled out, as the conditions called for at least ten. The "Sanspareil" made an average of fourteen miles an hour, but as it burst a water-pipe it lost its chance. The "Novelty" did splendidly, but also burst a pipe, and was crowded out, leaving the "Rocket" to carry off the honors with an average speed of fifteen miles an hour, the highest rate attained being twenty-nine. This was Stephenson's locomotive, and so fully vindicated his theory that the idea of stationary engines on a railroad was completely exploded. He had picked up the fixed engines which the genius of Watt had devised, and set them on wheels to draw men and merchandise, against the most direful predictions of the foremost engineers of his day.

[Footnote: See Smiles' "Life of George Stephenson" (new ed., 1874); Jeaffreson and Pole's "Life of Robert Stephenson" (1864), and article in Johnson's Cyclopedia, Vol. VII., p. 740.]

XV.

PROMPTNESS.

MEMORY GEMS.

One to-day is worth two to-morrows.—Franklin

Whilst we are considering when we are to begin, it is often too late to act.—Quintilian

By the street of by and by one arrives at the house of never.—Cervantes

When a fool makes up his mind, the market has gone by.—Spanish Proverb

The individual who is habitually tardy in meeting an appointment, will never be respected or successful in life.—W. Fisk

Promptness and punctuality are among the greatest blessings and comforts of life. For lack of these qualities, some of the greatest men have failed. Most men have abundant opportunities for promoting and securing their own happiness. Time should be made the most of. Stray moments, saved and improved, may yield many brilliant results. It is astonishing how much can be done by using up the odds and ends of time in leisure hours. We must be prompt to catch the minutes as they fly, and make them yield the treasures they contain, or they will be lost to us forever. "In youth the hours are golden, in mature years they are silvern, in old age they are leaden." "The man who at twenty knows nothing, at thirty does nothing, at forty has nothing." Yet the Italian proverb adds, "He who knows nothing is confident in everything."

In the most ordinary affairs of life we must take heed of the value of time, keep watch over it, and be punctual to others as well as to ourselves; for without punctuality, men are kept in a perpetual state of worry, trouble, and annoyance.

Webster was never late at a recitation in school or college. In court, in congress, in society, he was equally punctual. So, amid the cares and distractions of a singularly busy life, Horace Greeley managed to be on time for every appointment. Many a trenchant paragraph for the *Tribune* was written while the editor was waiting for men of leisure, tardy at some meeting.

John Quincy Adams was never known to be behind time. The Speaker of the House of Representatives knew when to call the House to order by seeing Mr. Adams coming to his seat. On one occasion a member said that it was time to begin. "No," said another, "Mr. Adams is not in his seat." It was found that the clock was three minutes fast, and prompt to the minute, Mr. Adams arrived.

Begin with promptness in little things. Be punctual at breakfast, even if you are sleepy. Be punctual at school, even if you have errands to do. Whatever you may have to do, think out the quickest way of doing it, and do it at once. By and by the habit becomes a quality of mind and action. Don't loiter about anything; it takes too much time.

We must be careful to remember that promptness is more than punctuality, which is an outward habit, and a very necessary one, if people live together. It is important also for one's own sake, even if he should be a Robinson Crusoe without a man Friday.

Promptness has to do with thought. It begins in learning how to think and reason. Behind it lies concentration, which first of all has made one thoroughly understand a subject. Then comes the second point,—what to do instantly in any given case; and the trained judgment ends in instant, wise action. When a boy saves another who has fallen through the ice, he unconsciously thought out long ago what to do when the moment came for him to act. When a girl throws a rug over the dress of her sister, which has caught fire, she knew long before what to do. This knowing what to do, and doing it, is called presence of mind, that is, having common sense all ready for use.

Promptness takes the drudgery out of an occupation. Putting off, usually means leaving off; and "going to do" becomes "going undone." Doing a deed is like sowing a seed; if not done at just the right time it will be forever out of season. The summer of eternity will not be long enough to bring to maturity the fruit of a delayed action.

Even in the old, slow days of stage-coaches, when it took a month of dangerous travel to accomplish the distance we can now cover in a few hours, unnecessary delay was a crime. One of the greatest gains civilization has made, is in the measuring and utilizing of time. We can do as much in an hour to-day as men could in twenty hours a hundred years ago; and if it was a hanging affair then to lose a few minutes, what should the penalty now be for a like offense?

One of the best things about school and college life is that the bell which strikes the hour for rising, for recitations, or for lectures, teaches habits of promptness. Every man should have a watch which is a good timekeeper; one that is "nearly right" encourages bad habits, and is an expensive investment at any price. Wear threadbare clothes, if you must, but never carry an inaccurate watch.

Some people are always a little too late, or a little too early, in everything they attempt. John B. Gough used to say "They have three hands apiece,—a right hand, a left hand, and a little behindhand." As boys, they were late at school, and unpunctual in their home duties. That was the way the habit was acquired; and now, when a responsibility claims them, they think that if they had only gone yesterday they would have obtained the situation, or they can probably get one to-morrow.

Delays often have dangerous endings. Colonel Rahl, the Hessian commander at Trenton, was playing cards when a messenger brought a letter stating that Washington was crossing the Delaware. He put the letter in his pocket without reading it, until the game was finished. He rallied his men only to die just before his troops were taken prisoners. Only a few minutes' delay, but it resulted in the loss of honor, liberty, and life.

Indecision becomes a disease, and procrastination is its forerunner. There is only one known remedy for the victims of indecision, and that is promptness. Otherwise the disease is fatal to all success or achievement. He who hesitates is lost. General Putnam was plowing, with his son Daniel, in eastern Connecticut, when the news of the battle of Lexington reached him. "He loitered not," said Daniel, "but left me, the driver of his team, to unyoke it in the furrow; and, not many days after, to follow him to camp."

The man who would forge to the front in this competitive age must be a man of prompt and determined decision. Like Cortes, he must burn his ships behind him, and make retreat forever impossible. When he draws his sword he must throw the scabbard away, lest in a moment of discouragement and irresolution he be tempted to sheath it. He must nail his colors to the mast, as Nelson did in battle, determined to sink with his ship if he cannot conquer. Prompt decision and sublime audacity have carried many a successful man over perilous crises where deliberation would have been ruin.

Henry IV, king of France, was another leader of remarkable promptness. His people said of him that "he wore out very little broadcloth, but a great deal of boot-leather," for he was always going from one place to another. In speaking of the Duc de Mayenne, Henry called him a great captain, but added, "I always have five hours the start of him." Getting ahead of time is as good a rule for boys and girls as for generals.

In our own country we have had generals who were especially noted for their dispatch. You know the story of "Sheridan's Ride" in the Shenandoah Valley. His men, thoroughly beaten for the moment, were fleeing before the Southerners, when he suddenly appeared, promptly decided to head them right about, and, by the inspiration of his single presence, turned defeat into victory.

Sailors must be even more prompt than soldiers, for in danger at sea not an instant can be lost. Not only must a sailor be prompt in action against storm, but he must be prompt with his sails in squally weather; he must be prompt with his helm when approaching land. Among the heroes of the sea, Lord Nelson is conspicuous for his prompt and courageous deeds. He had many faults; but England felt safe while he watched over her maritime affairs; for he was always beforehand, and never allowed himself to be surprised by misfortune.

It is so in the voyage of life. Incidents often occur which demand instantaneous action on our part; and these are the events which usually issue in failure or success. Prompt movement, at the right moment, is more valuable than rubies; and its lack often leads to utter ruin.

NAPOLEON BONAPARTE.

Napoleon changed the art of war quite as much by his promptness as by the concentration of his men in large masses. By his exceeding rapidity of movement he was long able to protect France against the combined powers of Europe. He was always quick to seize the advantages of an emergency. Though he can never be considered as the type of a noble man, he was an extraordinarily great man. Boys who like to read of battles, and trace the maneuvers of a campaign, will find that his military renown was largely due to his promptness.

Decision of purpose and rapidity of action enabled him to astonish the world with his marvelous successes. He appeared to be everywhere at once. What he could accomplish in a day, surprised all who knew him. He seemed to electrify everybody about him. His invincible energy thrilled the whole army. He could rouse to immediate and enthusiastic action the dullest troops, and inspire with courage the most stupid men. He would sit up all night, if necessary, after riding thirty or forty leagues, to attend to correspondence, dispatches and details. What a lesson his career affords to the shiftless and half-hearted!

There have been many times when a prompt decision, a rapid movement, an energetic action, have changed the very face of history; and, on the other hand, there have been many instances where the indecisions of generals, or the procrastination of subordinates, has cost thousands of precious lives, and the loss of millions of dollars worth of property.

Napoleon once invited his marshals to dine with him; but, as they did not arrive at the moment appointed, he began to eat without them. They came in just as he was rising from the table. "Gentlemen," said he, "it is now past dinner, and we will immediately proceed to business."

He laid great stress upon that "supreme moment," that "nick of time," which occurs in every battle; to take advantage of which means victory, and to lose in hesitation means disaster. He said that he beat the Austrians because they did not know the value of five minutes; and it has been said that, among the trifles that conspired to defeat him at Waterloo, the loss of a few minutes by himself and Grouchy on that fatal morning, was the most significant. Blucher was on time, and Grouchy was late. That may seem a small matter, but it was enough to bring Napoleon's career to a close, and to send him to St. Helena.

[Footnote: On Napoleon, see Seeley's "Short History of Napoleon I."; Ropes's "The First Napoleon," and articles in the current encyclopedias.]

XVI.

HONESTY.

MEMORY GEMS.

Truth needs no color, beauty no pencil.—Shakespeare

An honest man's the noblest work of God.—Pope

The basis of high thinking is perfect honesty.—Strong

Nature has written a letter of credit on some men's faces which is honored whenever presented.—Thackeray

If there were no honesty, it would be invented as a means of getting wealth.—Mirabeau

There are certain virtues and vices which very largely determine the happiness or the misery of every human life. Prominent among these virtues are those of truth and honesty; and to these are opposed the vices of lying and cheating.

Society is like a building, which stands firm when its foundations are strong and all its timbers are sound. The man who cannot be trusted is to society what a faulty foundation or a bit of rotten timber is to a house.

It is always mean for a man or boy "to go back," as we say, on a friend. It is still worse, if possible, to "go back" on one's self. A brave man or boy will manfully take the consequences of his acts, and if they are bad, will resolve to do better another time. The worst sort of deceit is that by which one lets another bear the blame, or in any way suffer, for what one has one's self done. Such meanness happens sometimes, but it is almost too bad to be spoken of.

There are certain kinds of cheating that the law cannot or does not touch. The man who practices this kind of dishonesty is even worse than if he were doing that which the law punishes. He uses the law, which was meant to protect society, as a cover from which he can attack society.

Lying is a form of dishonesty, and a very bad form of it. What would become of the world if we could not trust each other's word? A lie is always told for one of two ends; either to get some advantage to which one has no real claim, in which case it is merely a form of cheating; or to defend one's self from the bad consequences of something that one has done, in which case it is cowardly.

The Romans arranged the seats in their two temples to Virtue and Honor, so that no one could enter the second without passing through the first. Such is the order of advance,—Virtue, Toil, Honor.

The solid and useful virtue of honesty is highly practicable. "Nothing is profitable that is dishonest," is a truthful maxim. "Virtue alone is invincible." "I would give ten thousand dollars for your reputation for uprightness," said a sharper to an upright tradesman, "for I could make a hundred thousand dollars with it." Honesty succeeds, dishonesty fails. The honesty and integrity of A. T. Stewart won for him a great reputation, and the young schoolmaster who began life in New York on less than a dollar a day, amassed nearly forty million dollars, and there was not a smirched dollar in all those millions.

We do not count ourselves among those who believe that "every man has his price," and that "an honest man has a lock of hair growing in the palm of his right hand." No! There are in the world of business many more honest men than rogues, and for one trust betrayed there are thousands sacredly kept.

As a mere matter of selfishness, "honesty is the best policy." But he who is honest for policy's sake is already a moral bankrupt. Men of policy are honest when they think honesty will pay the better; but when policy will pay better they give honesty the slip. Honesty and policy have nothing in common. When policy is in, honesty is out. It is more honorable for some men to fail than for others to succeed. Part with anything rather than your integrity and conscious rectitude. Capital is not what a man has, but what a man is. Character is capital.

For example: A man wishes to succeed in business. His studies and his practical training have fitted him to do this. He seeks out all the methods by which he may reach success. He shrinks from no labor of mind, or, if need be, of body, for this end. In all this he is right. We admire skill, industry, and pluck. There is, however, one kind of means that he may not use. He may not stoop to fraud of any kind. He *may* desire and seek wealth; he *must* desire and seek honor and honesty. These are among the ends that morality insists upon, and that should not be sacrificed to anything else.

What contempt we have for a man who robs another, who picks his pocket, or knocks him down in some lonely place and strips him of whatever articles of value he may have. But the man who cheats is a thief, just as truly as the pickpocket and the highwayman.

There is nothing that improves a boy's character so much as putting him on his honor—trusting to his honor. We have little hope for the boy who is dead to the feeling of honor. The boy who needs to be continually looked after is on the road to ruin. If treating your boy as a gentleman does not make him a gentleman, nothing else will.

There are many incidents in Abraham Lincoln's career which illustrate this virtue; and from these we select the following: While tending store, Lincoln once sold to a woman goods to the amount of two dollars, six and a quarter cents. He discovered later that a mistake had been made, and that the store owed the customer the six and a quarter cents. After he had closed the store that night, he walked several miles in the darkness to return the amount.

At another time a woman bought a pound of tea. Lincoln discovered the next morning that a smaller weight was on the scales. He at once weighed out the remainder, and walked some distance before breakfast to return it.

He was once a postmaster in New Salem; but the office was finally discontinued. Several years after, the agent called at his law office, and presented a claim of about seventeen dollars in the settlement of the New Salem affairs. Mr. Lincoln took out a little trunk, and produced the exact sum, wrapped in a linen rag. It had lain there untouched through years of the greatest hardship and self-denial. He said, "I never use any one's money but my own."

Honor lies in doing well whatever we find to do; and the world estimates a man's abilities in accordance with his success in whatever business or profession he may engage. The true gentleman is known by his strict sense of honor; by his sympathy, his gentleness, his forbearance, and his generosity. He is essentially a man of truth, speaking and doing rightly, not merely in the sight of men, but in his secret and private behavior. Truthfulness is moral transparency. Hence the gentleman promises nothing that he has not the means of performing. The Duke of Wellington proudly declared that truth was the characteristic of an English officer, that when he was bound by a parole he would not break his word; for the gentleman scorns to lie, in word or deed; and is ready to brave all consequences rather than debase himself by falsehood.

When any one complains, as Diogenes did, that he has to hunt the streets with candles at noonday to find an honest man, we are apt to think that his nearest neighbor would have quite as much difficulty in making such a discovery. If you think there is not a true man living, you had better, for appearance's sake, not say so until you are dead yourself.

A few years since, a manly boy about nine years old stepped up to a gentleman in the Grand Central Depot, New York, and asked, "Shine, sir?" "Yes I want my shoes blacked," said the gentleman. "Then I would be glad to shine them, sir," said the boy. "Have I time to catch the Hudson River train?" "No time to lose, sir; but I can give you a good job before it pulls out. Shall I?" "Yes, my boy; but don't let me be left."

In two seconds the bootblack was on his knees and hard at work. "The train is going, sir," said the boy, as he gave the last touch. The gentleman gave the boy a half dollar, and started for the train. The boy counted out the change and ran after the gentleman, but was too late, for the train was gone.

Two years later the same gentleman, coming to New York, met the bootblack, but had forgotten him. The boy remembered the gentleman, and asked him, "Didn't I shine your shoes once in the Grand Central Depot?" "Some boy did," said the man. "I am the boy, and here is your change, sir." The gentleman was so pleased with the lad's honesty, that he went with him to see his mother, and offered to adopt him, as he needed such a boy. The mother consented, and the honest bootblack had after that a good home. He was given a good education, and, when a man, became a partner in the gentleman's large business.

GEORGE PEABODY.

At eleven years of age George Peabody had to go out into the world to earn his living. His promptness and honesty won for him the esteem of his employer. At the age of fifteen he was left fatherless, without a dollar in the world. An uncle in Georgetown, D. C., hearing that the boy needed work, sent for him and gave him employment. His genial manner and respectful bearing gained him many friends. He never wounded the feelings of the buyer of goods, never seemed impatient, and was strictly honest in all his dealings. His energy, perseverance, and honesty made him a partner in the business when only nineteen years of age. At the age of thirty-five he became the head of a large and wealthy business, which his own industry had helped to build. He had bent his life to one purpose, to make his business a success.

Having visited London several times in matters of trade, he determined to make that city his place of residence. In 1837, there came a great business panic in the United States. Many banks suspended specie payments. Many mercantile houses went to the wall, and thousands more were in great distress. Faith in the credit of the United States was almost lost. Probably not one half dozen men in Europe would have been listened to for a moment in the Bank of England upon the subject of American securities, but George Peabody was one of them.

He became a wealthy man, honored at home and abroad. He loved his fellow-men and set himself the task of relieving their wants. He gave ten thousand dollars to help fit out the second expedition for the relief of Sir John Franklin. The same year, his native town of Danvers, Massachusetts, celebrated its centennial. The rich London banker was of course invited. He was too busy to be present but sent a letter. The seal was broken at dinner, and this was the toast it contained:

"Education—a debt due from present to future generations." In the same envelope was a check for twenty thousand dollars for a town library and institute. At another banquet given in his honor at Danvers, years afterward, he gave two hundred and fifty thousand dollars to the same institute. Edward

Everett, and others, made eloquent addresses, and then the kind-faced, great-hearted man responded.

"There is not a youth within the sound of my voice whose early opportunities and advantages are not very much better than were mine. I have achieved nothing that is impossible to the most humble boy among you. Steadfast and undeviating *truth*, fearless and straight forward integrity, and an honor ever unsullied by an unworthy word or action, make their possessor greater than worldly success."

[Footnote: See the life of George Peabody, by Phebe A. Hanaford (Boston, 1882), and numerous articles in the cyclopedias and magazines.]

XVII.

COURTESY.

MEMORY GEMS.

Conduct is three fourths of life.—Matthew Arnold

There is no policy like politeness.—Magoon

Life is not so short but there is time enough for courtesy.—Emerson

Men, like bullets, go farthest when they are smoothest.—Richter

Nothing can constitute good breeding that has not good-nature for its foundation.—Bulwer

True courtesy consists in that gentle refinement and grace of manner displayed toward others, which springs not so much from polite culture as from a genuine goodness of heart. It is the honor due to man as man, and especially to woman. It is a grace which is too often unrecognized and undervalued; but, when of the true order, it is a jewel of great price.

It is to be found in all lands, and in every grade or order of society, as shown by the following examples:

A Chinaman was rudely pushed into the mud by an American. He picked himself up very calmly, shook off some of the mud, bowed very politely, and said in a mild, reproving tone of voice, "You Christian; me heathen; alle samee, good-bye." Courtesy, as a Christian duty, has been sorely neglected by Americans. "If a civil word or two will make a man happy," said a French king, "he must be wretched indeed who will not give them to him."

The first Duke of Marlborough "wrote English badly and spelled it worse," yet he swayed the destinies of empires. The charm of his manner was irresistible and influenced all Europe. His fascinating smile and winning speech disarmed the fiercest hatred, and made friends of the bitterest enemies.

A habit of courtesy is like a delicate wrapping, preventing one personality from rubbing and chafing against another. It is perhaps most of all proper from the young toward those who are older than themselves. There is too little of this in our day. Boys and girls speak to their elders, perhaps even to their parents, with rude familiarity, such as would be hardly proper among playmates.

One should also show courtesy to his companions. Boys, even in their play, should be courteous to one another. One who is always pushing for the best, without regard to others, shows his ill breeding. A "thank you" and a "please" on proper occasions, are not out of place even among the closest companions.

Perhaps in the family, courtesy is more important than anywhere else. There people are thrown more closely together; and, thus, nowhere do they need more the protection of courtesy. From all this, it appears that courtesy is simply an expression of thoughtfulness for others; and that rudeness and boorishness, though sometimes they spring from ignorance, are more often the expression of selfishness, which forgets the feelings and the tastes of others.

When Edward Everett took a professor's chair at Harvard, after five years of study in Europe, he was almost worshiped by the students. His manner seemed touched by that exquisite grace seldom found except in women of rare culture. His great popularity lay in a courteous and magnetic atmosphere which every one felt, but no one could fully describe, and which never left him throughout his long and useful life.

Courtesy, then, may be defined as "good manners." At present we use the word "manners," simply to express the outward relations of life. We speak of "good manners" or "bad manners," meaning by the words that a person conforms more or less perfectly to what are called the "usages of good society." Thus a man may have good morals and bad manners, or he may have good manners and bad morals, or both his manners and his morals may be either good or bad.

Etiquette originally meant the ticket or tag tied to a bag to indicate its contents. If a bag had this ticket it was not examined. From this the word passed to cards upon which were printed certain rules to be observed by guests. These rules were "the ticket" or the etiquette. To be "the ticket," or, as it was sometimes expressed, "to act or talk by the card," became the thing with the better classes.

A fine manner more than compensates for all the defects of nature. The most fascinating person is always the one of most winning manners, not the one of greatest physical beauty. The Greeks thought beauty was a proof of the peculiar favor of the gods, and considered that beauty only worth adorning and transmitting which was unmarred by outward manifestations of hard and haughty feeling. According to their ideal, beauty must be the expression of attractive qualities within—such as cheerfulness, benignity, contentment, and love.

On a certain occasion, Queen Victoria sent for Thomas Carlyle, who was a Scotch peasant, offering him the title of nobleman, which he declined, feeling that he had always been a nobleman in his own right. He understood so little of the manners at court that, when presented to the queen, after speaking to her a few minutes, being tired, he said, "Let us sit down, madam, and talk it over;" whereat the courtiers were ready to faint. But the queen was equal to the occasion and gave a gesture that seated all her attendants in a moment.

Courtesy is not, however, always found in high places. Even royal courts furnish many examples of bad manners. At an entertainment given by the Prince of Wales, to which, of course, only the very cream of society was admitted, there was such pushing and struggling to see the Princess, who was then but recently married, that, as she passed through the reception rooms, a bust of the princess Eoyal was thrown from its pedestal and damaged, and the pedestal upset; and the ladies, in their eagerness to see the princess, actually stood upon it.

Courtesy does not necessarily conflict with sincerity. It is a great mistake to suppose that righteousness is bound up with bluntness and criticism. Perfect courtesy and perfect honesty are often combined in the same person. We can be amiable without being weak. We are able to criticise errors and wrongs by holding up what is right and true, which is the most forcible way; and still, through it all, our gentleness and courtesy may remain unstained.

Where this course is departed from, we are very apt to fall into trouble. A New York lady had just taken her seat in a car on a train bound for Philadelphia, when a somewhat stout man sitting just ahead of her lighted a cigar. She coughed and moved uneasily; but the hints had no effect, so she said tartly: "You probably are a foreigner, and do not know that there is a smoking-car attached to the train. Smoking is not permitted here." The man made no reply, but threw his cigar out of the window. What was her astonishment when the conductor told her, a moment after, that she had entered the private car of General Grant. She withdrew in confusion, but the same line courtesy which led him to give up his cigar, was shown again as he spared her the mortification of even a questioning glance, still less of a look of amusement, although she watched his dumb, immovable figure with apprehension until she reached the door.

Let us not be so busy as to forget the gracious acts and delicate courtesies of everyday life. As Dr. Bartol says: "These friendly good-mornings, these ownings of mutual ties, take on, in their mass, a character of the sublime. The young owe respect to their elders. There is a great deal of affection shown in our day, but the expression of reverence is not so common. Good manners are not simply 'a fortune' to a young person; they are more. They constitute the proof of a noble character."

RALPH WALDO EMERSON.

In selecting Ralph Waldo Emerson as our special example, we are sure of an admirable illustration. He was born in Boston, Massachusetts, on the 25th of

May, 1803, the second of five sons. His father was the Rev. William Emerson, minister of the First Church, in Boston. One of his schoolmates says that as a youth, "it was impossible that there should be any feeling about him but of regard and affection." His course and graduation at Harvard College are remembered by his friends as marked chiefly by amiability, meditation, and faultless conduct. He taught school a short time and "made all the boys love him"; holding perfect control beneath courteous manners.

Later on Emerson entered the ministry and became pastor of a church in Boston. He was greatly beloved by all who knew him. The cause of this universal affection was not solely in the books he produced, but in the wonderful courtesy of his character, as it faced toward life in every relation.

His son, Edward W. Emerson, says: "My father's honor for humanity, and respect for humble people and for labor, were strong characteristics. To servants, he was kindly and delicately considerate; always fearful lest their feelings might be wounded. He built his own fires, going to the woodpile in the yard in all weather for armfuls of wood as occasion required." He then adds, "Nothing could be better than his manner to children and young people; affectionate, and with a marked respect for their personality."

Never patronizing, always appreciative, he touched everybody with courtesy, and was, as Matthew Arnold said, "The friend of those who live in the spirit of high, generous standards." We see in his example what deep, real courtesy is. Courtesy, to him, was sincerity, and fairness, and good-will, all round. He welcomed shy merit, encouraged clumsyyouth, and smiled on good intentions, however poorly expressed. He did all this day after day at the cost of time and patience and strength. As a scholar, he might have secluded himself and simply written great books; but the power he is, and is to be, could not have been obtained that way.

[Footnote: See "Ralph Waldo Emerson," by O. W. Holmes (Boston, 1884); "Emerson at Home and Abroad," by H. D. Conway; and F. B. Sanborn's "Homes and Haunts of Emerson."]

XVIII.

SELF-DENIAL.

MEMORY GEMS.

Self-denial is the essence of heroism.—Emerson

True self-denial involves personal sacrifice for the good of others.
—Dr. Momerie

To give up interest for duty is the alphabet of morals.—James Hinton

A man of self-denial has the true ring which distinguishes the genuine from the counterfeit.—Prof. Seeley

The worst education which teaches self-denial is better than the best which teaches everything else, and not that.—John Sterling

It is a mistake to imagine that self-sacrifice and self-denial are precisely the same. Many persons seem to think that because self-sacrifice is a noble thing, everything in which self is given up must be noble. Self may sometimes be sacrificed when it ought to be maintained; and sometimes we sacrifice our interest to save ourselves a little trouble, or to get rid of some petty annoyance. We say, "Well, I have a right to do this, but, let it go;" and then we fancy that we have performed a noble deed, whereas, we have really been serving our own selfishness and love of ease.

True self-denial is the result of a calm and deliberate attachment to the highest good, and consists in the giving up of everything which stands in the way of its attainment, no matter what it may cost us either in suffering or loss.

In our earliest years we must train ourselves to forego little things for the sake of others. If we do so, we shall find it much easier to bear the heavier disappointments of maturer years. It will greatly help us if we try to practice at least one distinct act of self-denial every day; and we must not forget that these acts must be both voluntary and cheerful if they are to be of real benefit either to ourselves or to others.

The burdens which boyhood and girlhood must bear in acquiring an education, learning a trade, resisting temptations, and building spotless characters, demand the constant exercise of self-denial. Many people, young and old, know what duty is, but fail to do it for the want of decision. They know very well what labors and self-denials are necessary to obtain an education, master a trade, or attain to excellence in any pursuit; but their ignoble indecision, which is a sort of mental and moral debility, disqualifies them for the undertaking. "The will, which is the central force of character, must be trained to habits of decision; otherwise, it will neither be able to resist evil, nor to follow good."

Our subject brings to mind many heroes of all kinds, to whose lives we would gladly refer, if our space permitted. They are found in all stations of life. There have been railway engineers, who, when they saw that a collision could not be avoided, have stood at their place to lighten, if possible, the shock, and have been killed; sea captains, who have remained at their posts till all others had left, and have gone down with their ships; physicians and nurses, and sisters of charity, who have not shrunk from pestilence in order to save life, or to comfort the dying. There was Father Damien, a Catholic priest, who so pitied the lepers that were confined to an island, deprived alike of the comforts of this world and of the consolations of religion, that he went and lived with them. He knew that when he once joined them he would probably take their disease, and, in any case, could never leave them. But he went, shared their lot, lived and died among them; seeking to do them good.

Historic illustrations of self-denial, still fresh in the memories of many citizens, are to the point here. General Grant had been for several months in front of Petersburg, apparently accomplishing nothing, while General Sherman had captured Atlanta, and completed his grand "march to the sea." Then arose a strong cry to promote Sherman to Grant's position as lieutenant-general. Hearing of it, Sherman wrote to Grant:

"I have written to John Sherman [his brother] to stop it. I would rather have you in command than any one else. I should emphatically decline any commission calculated to bring us into rivalry."

General Grant replied:

"No one would be more pleased with your advancement than I; and if you should be placed in my position, and I put subordinate, it would not change our relations in the least. I would make the same exertions to support you, that you have done to support me; and I would do all in my power to make our cause win."

Two great souls striving to be equally magnanimous! Could anything be more beautiful or noble in public life, where jealousy, and selfishness and double-dealing appear to rule the hour?

One or two other illustrations must suffice us. The captain of a ship was absent from it one day, being on board another vessel. While he was gone, a storm arose, which in a short time made an entire wreck of his own ship, to which it had not been possible for him to return. He had left on board two little boys, the one four years old and the other six, under the care of a young colored servant. The people struggled to get out of the sinking ship into a large boat; and the poor servant took the captain's two little children, tied them in a sack, and put them into the boat, which was by this time quite full. He was stepping into it himself, but was told by the officer that there was no room forhim,— that either he or the children must perish, for the weight of all would sink the boat. The heroic servant did not hesitate a moment. "Very well," said he; "give my love to my master, and tell him I beg pardon for all my faults;" and then he went to the bottom, never to rise again till the sea shall give up its dead.

The power and influence of self-denial are well set forth in the following incident:

At a time of great scarcity in Germany, a certain rich man invited twenty poor children to his house, and said to them, "In this basket there is a loaf of bread for each of you; take it, and come again every day at this hour until the coming of better times."

The children seized upon the basket, wrangled and fought for the bread, as each wished to get the best and largest loaf; and at last they went away without even thanking him.

Frances alone, a poor but neatly dressed child, stood modestly at a distance, took the smallest loaf that was left in the basket, thanked the gentleman, and went home in a quiet and orderly manner.

On the following day the children were just as ill-behaved; and poor Frances this time received a loaf which was scarcely half the size of the rest; but when she came home, and her mother began to cut the bread, there fell out of it a number of bright new silver coins.

Her mother was perplexed and said, "Take back the money this instant; for it has no doubt, got into the bread through some mistake."

Frances carried it back. But the benevolent man said, "No, no! it was no mistake. I had the money baked in the smallest loaf in order to reward you, my dear child. Remember that the person who is contented with the smallest loaf, rather than quarrel for the largest one, will find blessings still more valuable than money baked in bread."

All these incidents reveal the value of this trait in real life; and also serve to show how it is regarded by others than ourselves. It will more than repay us for its cultivation, both by the increase of our own happiness, and in the large amount of enjoyment it will put into the lives of those about us.

CHARLES LAMB.

Charles Lamb was a writer of charming essays, full of wit and fancy. He seemed to the world as far as possible from a hero; yet his life washeroic in an unusual degree.

He was the son of a clerk in the London Law Courts, and the youngest child in a family of three. He had a brother, John, who was twelve years, and a sister Mary, ten years older than himself. At the age of seventeen he became a clerk in the Accountant's Office of the East India Company. There was a kind of insanity in the family, and in September, 1796, Charles Lamb came home from his office-work to find that his sister had wounded her father in the forehead and had stabbed her mother to the heart. The inquest on the mother, held next day, was closed with a verdict of insanity, and Mary Lamb was placed in a lunatic asylum.

John Lamb, the elder brother, offered no aid to the family. Charles loved his sister, and cared for her with a beautiful devotion. The combined earnings of Charles and his father were less than two hundred pounds a year, but Charles so arranged matters that sixty pounds a year was devoted to her support. Others of the family, especially her brother John, opposed Mary's discharge from the asylum; but Charles obtained her release by solemnly promising that he would take care of her.

Although he was engaged to be married to a woman whom he tenderly loved, he gave up all for Mary's sake, and literally filled her life with his love. First he placed her in a lodging at Hackney, and spent all his Sundays and holidays with her. Then they lived together; he watching the moods that foreshadowed a mad fit, and taking her when needful, a willing patient, to the Hoxton asylum till the fit was over. It was a sad sight to see the brother and sister walking across the fields to the hospital together, when she felt that the trouble was coming on; but through the long period of forty years his love never once failed, and his devotion increased to the very end.

His whole life developed into one of singular kindness and self-sacrifice. He is known to have worn a coat six months longer than he otherwise would have done, in order that he might spare a little money to help some one less fortunate than himself. One of his many friends, speaking of him said, "Of all the men of genius I ever knew, the one most intensely and universally to be loved was Charles Lamb."

[Footnote: See Hazlitt's "Mary and Charles Lamb" (1874); "Biography of Charles Lamb," T. N. Talfourd (1840); and "Final Memoirs," T. N. Talfourd (1848).]

XIX.

SELF-RESPECT.

MEMORY GEMS.

Above all things reverence yourself.—Pythagoras

No one can disgrace us but ourselves.—J. G. Holland

Self-distrust is the cause of most of our failures.—Bovee

Self-reverence, self-knowledge, self-control, these three alone lead
    life to sovereign power.—Tennyson

To thine own self be true; and it will follow, as night the day, thou
    canst not then be false to any man.—Shakespeare

There is around every man or woman, every boy or girl, a certain atmosphere
that keeps him or her separate and distinct from all other persons. We realize
the truth of this statement very early in life; and unless we can learn to respect
and rely upon our own distinctive self-hood, our lives will never reach their
largest possibilities.

There is, however, a real difference between self-reliance and self-respect,
though each partakes of the nature of the other. Self-respect is the root of
which self-reliance is the growth in various acts or plans. It is the general tone
and spirit running through our view of life, of our nature, of our friends, of
our privileges, of our personal gifts. It is the basis on which we build self-
reliant conduct and self-reliant convictions.

It is generally the man who thinks well of himself who comes to be thought
well of. But it is also true that when a man becomes perfectly satisfied with
himself and his worldly surroundings, he has reached the first stage of
decline. Self-confidence, backed by good common sense, is one of the most
important of human attributes. But we must be careful not to exaggerate
ourselves, or rate ourselves too highly. There are dangers attending every
virtue. Pushed to excess, even conscience, justice, and earnestness, may
become injurious. Self-respect must be guarded by common sense, love of
humanity, and the spirit of reverence. But nothing can make good an absence
of this quality.

Even the Chinese say, "It never pays to respect a man who does not respect
himself." If the world sees that you do not honor yourself, it has a right to
reject you as an impostor; because you claim to be worthy of the good
opinion of others when you have not your own. Self-respect is based upon
the same principles as respect for others. The scales of justice hang in every

heart, and even the murderer respects the judge who condemns him; for the still small voice within says, "That is right."

Self-respect is a great aid to pure living. So long as a youth has true self-respect, vice has little attraction for him. It is when this sterling virtue is sacrificed, and the thoughtless or reckless one ceases to care what is thought of him, that vice claims its victim. He who cares not whether men think well or ill of him, does not possess self-respect; and so he is easily lured into evil, becoming more and more indifferent to the good-will of others, and more thoughtless and abandoned in his daily life. With the loss of self-respect, he is likely to lose all that makes manhood true and noble.

The key to John Bunyan's career is found in the self-respect which began to govern his thoughts and acts in maturing youth, and which afterward enabled him to meet persecution victoriously and to develop his peculiar talent. If lie had been turned back by the scorn and contempt heaped upon him on account of his low condition, or if he had listened to critics who laughed at his simple, direct style in "Pilgrim's Progress"; or if he had lost courage because he belonged to a despised religious sect; we should never have had his inspiring example.

The main business of life is not to do something great, but to become great in ourselves. Any action has its finest and most enduring fruit in character. Men of character are the conscience of the society to which they belong. They, rather than the police, guarantee the execution of the laws. Their influence is the bulwark of good government.

Character gravitates upward, while mere genius, without character, gravitates downward. How often we see, in school or college, young men, who are apparently dull and even stupid, rise gradually and surely above others who are without character, merely because the former have an upward tendency in their lives, a reaching-up principle, which gradually but surely unfolds and elevates them to positions of honor and trust. There is something which everybody admires in an aspiring soul, one whose tendency is upward and onward, in spite of hindrances and in defiance of obstacles.

As illustrating the mighty results of character based upon a self-respecting love of honor, we may relate that when General Lee was in conversation with one of his officers in regard to a movement of his army, a plain farmer's boy overheard the general's remark that he had decided to march upon Gettysburg instead of Harrisburg. The boy telegraphed this fact to Governor Curtin. A special engine was sent for the boy. "I would give my right hand," said the governor, "to know if this boy tells the truth." A corporal replied, "Governor, I know that boy; it is impossible for him to lie; there is not a drop of false blood in his veins." In fifteen minutes the Union troops were marching to Gettysburg, where they gained a glorious victory.

True self-respect challenges the admiration of others. No man has reason to claim the regard of his fellows unless he first respects himself, for this latter act is the outcome of the only elements of character that can command the sincere esteem of men. A mean man, a dishonest man, a niggardly man, a lazy man, or a conceited man, does not respect himself. Unless he is living under the power of some strong delusion, he knows that he is not worthy of regard.

A young man was invited by a friend to attend an entertainment which he thought was objectionable. "I am not entirely clear that it is wrong," he said, "and when I am in doubt, I think the safer course is to decline."

"Perhaps you are right," answered the friend; "but I think that people will respect you as much as ever if you go."

"Possibly; but I want to respect myself," replied the young man. "I should lose my self-respect by performing a doubtful act. My aim should be higher than that."

Samuel Smiles expresses the truth well in this extract from "Character": "It is the great lesson of biography to teach what man can be and can do at his best. It may thus give each man renewed strength and confidence. The humblest, in sight of even the greatest, may admire and hope and take courage. These great brothers of ours in blood and lineage, who live a universal life, still speak to us from their graves, and beckon us on in the paths which they have trod."

One of the last things said by Sir Walter Scott, as he lay dying, was this: "I have been, perhaps, the most voluminous author of my day, and it is a comfort to me to think that I have tried to unsettle no man's faith, to corrupt no man's principles, and that I have written nothing which, on my deathbed, I would wish blotted out." To have lived such a life as he lived is more than to have reigned over a kingdom.

SIR WALTER SCOTT.

We are glad to call special attention to Scott, because of his heroic struggle to maintain his good name. He was born in Edinburgh, August 15, 1771. He was the son of Walter Scott, an attorney at law; and Anne Rutherford, daughter of Dr. John Rutherford, professor of medicine in the University of Edinburgh, and a lineal descendant from the ancient chieftain Walter Scott, traditionally known as "Auld Walt of Harden."

As a schoolboy Walter was very popular. He made himself respected for his courage and general ability to take care of himself. He was not considered a very bright scholar, although, even then, he gave evidence of his special delight in history, poetry, fairy tales, and fables. In 1783 he entered the university. He made little progress in the ancient languages, but was more successful in other studies. His time, however, was industriously employed in storing his mind with that great wealth of knowledge which afterward made him famous as a writer.

Scott was educated for a lawyer, but all his natural tastes were in the direction of literature. The greater part of his early life was an unconscious preparation for writing. He had been writing prose romances for several years with considerable success, when in January, 1805, he published "The Lay of the Last Minstrel." It at once became extremely popular. It sold more widely than any poem had ever sold before. This led him to decide that literature was to be the main business of his life. "Marmion," which appeared in 1808, and "The Lady of the Lake," in 1810, placed Scott among the greatest living poets. He touched then the highest point of happiness and prosperity.

Soon after this he entered into a business partnership with a publishing house, which resulted in his financial ruin. The failure left him partner to a debt of over one hundred thousand pounds. At the age of fifty-five, when all the freshness of youth was gone, he set himself the task of paying this enormous claim and winning back his ancestral estates. He went to work with a dogged determination to pay off his debt of honor. The heaviest blow was to his pride; yet pride alone never enabled any man to struggle so vigorously to meet the obligations he had incurred. It was rather that high feeling of self-respect which nerved his power to meet and try to overcome his great misfortune. His estates were conveyed to trustees for the benefit of his creditors, until such time as he could free them. Between January, 1826, and January, 1828, he earned forty thousand pounds by unremitting toil. Then his health broke down; yet he still struggled on with enfeebled constitution, but with an unbroken will, to discharge, if possible, his obligations, and leave to the world a respected name.

[Footnote: See Lockhart's "Life of Sir Walter Scott" (Houghton, Mifflin & Co.); Hutton's "Sir Walter Scott;" and articles in encyclopedias.]

XX.

CONSCIENTIOUSNESS.

MEMORY GEMS.

Conscientiousness is the underlying granite of life.—Sir Walter Raleigh

When love of praise takes the place of praiseworthiness, the defect is fatal.—S. Baring-Gould

When a man is dead to the sense of right, he is lost forever.
—James McCrie

Insincerity alienates love and rots away authority.—Bulwer

The value of conscientiousness is principally seen in the benefits of civilization.—Charles Kingsley

"Conscientiousness is a scrupulous regard to the decisions of conscience." When we say a duty was performed "religiously," it is the same as a duty done conscientiously. Conscience does not *teach* us what is right; we learn that from experience, and in many other ways. It simply tells us to do the best we know, and reproaches us when we do otherwise.

Some one has well said: "We can train ourselves to be conscientious, to be responsive to conscience, to obey it; but conscience itself cannot be educated. It is like the sun. We may so arrange our house as to receive the largest amount of sunlight; but the sun itself cannot be changed either for our advantage or disadvantage. As a house with ample windows is illuminated within by the rays of the sun, so is a well-trained life filled with the light of conscience." We may therefore define conscientiousness as the inborn desire to do that which is right and just.

Conscientiousness, which is, as we have just seen, another name for justice, is a trait to be cultivated among young people in their sports, in family life, and in school. A boy is unjust who refuses to "play fair"; a girl is unjust who deprives a friend of anything properly hers. Young people may be unjust in their words, in their thoughts, or in their actions; and the greatest watchfulness is needed to prevent us from failing in this important matter.

One's sense of justice may be increased by thoughtfulness as to his duty to himself, as well as to others; and by demanding very rigid observance of every law of conduct which commends itself as needful to ideal character. "There is only one real failure possible in life," said Canon Farrar, "and that is, not to be true to the best one knows."

"I can remember when you blackened my father's shoes," said one member of the British House of Commons to another in the heat of debate. "True enough," was the prompt reply, "but did I not blacken them well?" The sense of right-doing was sufficient to turn an intended insult into a well-merited compliment, and to increase for him the esteem of his fellow-members.

"Whatever is right to do," said an eminent writer, "should be done with our best care, strength, and faithfulness of purpose."

Leonardo da Vinci would walk across Milan to change a single tint or the slightest detail in his famous picture of "The Last Supper."

Rufus Choate would plead before a shoemaker justice of the peace, in a petty case, with all the fervor and careful attention to detail with which he addressed the United States Supreme Court.

"No, I can't do it, it is impossible," said Webster, when pressed to speak on a question soon to come up, toward the close of a Congressional session. "I am so pressed with other duties that I haven't time to prepare myself to speak upon that theme." "Ah, but Mr. Webster, you always speak well upon any subject. You never fail." "But that's the very reason," said the orator, "because I never allow myself to speak upon any subject without first making that subject thoroughly my own. I haven't time to do that in this instance. Hence I must refuse."

Among the list of our great reformers, William Lloyd Garrison must always hold a very prominent place. The work he did was that of unselfish devotion to an overmastering sense of justice. He labored for those in bonds, as bound with them. Faithful, as but few others were faithful, he worked in season and out of season for human freedom. After great effort, Mr. Garrison succeeded in establishing an antislavery society, and he was made its agent to lecture for the cause. He was sent to England to solicit funds for starting a manual-labor school for the colored youth. But the whole tone of society was against him. He was at the mercy of that prejudice which, at so many points, was ready to adopt mob violence. The discussion of slavery was taken up in educational institutions where, as in general society, but very few were found who believed in universal freedom. But still he never swerved from what he believed to be right. Justice was his plea; justice was his battle cry; and it came to be said of him that "He was conscience incarnated."

A beautiful illustration of justice, and fairness of treatment, occurred at the opening of the great battle of Manila Bay, on May 1, 1898.

When the order was given to strip for action, one of the powder boys tore his coat off hurriedly, and it fell from his hands and went over the rail, down into the bay. A few moments before, he had been gazing on his mother's photograph, and just before he took his coat off he had kissed the picture and put it in his inside pocket. When the coat fell overboard he turned to the captain and asked permission to jump over and get it. Naturally the request was refused. The boy then went to the other side of the ship and climbed down the ladder. He swam around to the place where the coat had dropped and succeeded in getting it. When he came back he was put in irons for disobedience. After the battle he was tried by a court-martial for disobedience, and found guilty.

Commodore Dewey became interested in the case, for he could not understand why the boy had risked his life and disobeyed orders for a coat. The lad had never told his motives. But when the commodore talked to him in a kindly way, and asked him why he had done such a strange thing for an old coat, he burst into tears and told the commodore that his mother's picture was in the coat. Dewey's eyes filled with tears as he listened to the story. Then he picked up the boy and embraced him. He ordered the little fellow to be instantly released and pardoned. "A boy who loves his mother enough to risk his life for her picture, cannot be kept in irons on this fleet," he said.

Examples by the score crowd in upon our minds as we think more deeply into this subject, but space permits of only one more before passing to our special illustration:

When troubled with deafness, the Duke of Wellington consulted a celebrated physician, who put strong caustic into his ear, causing an inflammation which threatened his life. The doctor apologized, expressed great regrets, and said that the blunder would ruin him. "No," said Wellington, "I will never mention it." "But will you allow me to attend you, so that the people will not withdraw their confidence?" "No," said the Iron Duke, "that would be lying."

Enough has perhaps been said to show that conscientiousness and justice are not simply beautiful traits of character; but that they are absolutely necessary to the fullest advancement of the individual and of the race. We proceed to enforce this truth still more strongly, however, by a closing reference to the career of one of our greatest statesmen.

CHARLES SUMNER.

In using Mr. Sumner as our special illustration of conscientiousness, it is not because we lack other examples. On the contrary, they are all about us; and doubtless we could all mention excellent cases in our own homes, and among our own acquaintances, where conscientiousness has been vividly illustrated. He was the eldest of nine children, and was born in Boston, on the sixth day of January, 1811. His father was a lawyer, and sheriff of Suffolk County, and was descended from the early colonists of New England. Even in childhood and youth Charles Sumner evinced the quiet, thoughtful, and serious temperament which was characteristic of the Puritans. As a boy he took little interest in games and frolics. He read much, and was reserved and awkward.

Society to him, in early life, possessed no attractions; and while he was always studious and patient he never displayed any marked talent.

His progress in life was almost entirely due to his conscientious, persistent, untiring application to the acquisition of knowledge and the development of all his powers. He was in the highest sense a cultivated man. His mind became, through conscientious and laborious study, a great storehouse, filled with the richest materials and the power to use them.

But he did not seek these treasures of learning and power for the simple end of glorifying himself. His one great object in life was to benefit mankind. He said in an address, delivered just after he had begun the practice of law, speaking of conscience and charity: "They must become a part of us and of our existence, as present, in season and out of season, in all the amenities of life, in those daily offices of conduct and manner which add so much to its charm, as also in those grander duties whose performance evinces an ennobling self-sacrifice." It was his own determined and unfaltering devotion to this lofty ideal, that led directly to the success of his great public career.

Charles Sumner was first elected to the Senate in 1851. Throughout his brilliant life his lofty character never forsook him; and if we will carefully examine the measures which he advocated, voted for, or opposed, from time to time, the discovery will be made that his conscience was his inevitable guide.

While he dearly loved peace, he was always in the midst of warfare. He constantly incurred the censure which arises from advocating unpopular measures. Childlike in his personal friendships, he often spoke about himself as he would speak of others,—revealing what others would have concealed. Frank, sincere, and pledged from youth to principles, rather than to persons, he was obliged to struggle against great obstacles. To him the slave was a human being with a soul, entitled to every right and privilege accorded to any American citizen. He devoted his energies to the cause of freedom down to the very last, and died in Washington, on March 11, 1874, exclaiming, "Don't let my Civil Rights Bill fail!"

[Footnote: See "Memoir and Letters of Charles Sumner," by Edward L. Pierce, (Boston, 1877), and many articles in the magazines, especially noting the sketch in Appleton's Cyclopedia of American Biography, Vol. V., page 744.]

XXI.

ENTHUSIASM.

MEMOBY GEMS.

Nothing is so contagious as enthusiasm.—Bulwer

Enthusiasm is the fundamental quality of strong souls.—Carlyle

The only conclusive evidence of a man's sincerity is that he gives himself for a principle.—Phillips Brooks

Enthusiasm is the romance of the boy that becomes the heroism of the man.—A. Bronson Alcott

Every great and commanding movement in the annals of the world is the triumph of some enthusiasm.—Emerson

In the course of every life there are sure to be obstacles and difficulties to be met. Prudence hesitates and examines them; intelligence usually suggests some ingenious way of getting around them; patience and perseverance deliberately go to work to dig under them; but enthusiasm is the quality that boldly faces and leaps lightly over them. By the power of enthusiasm the most extraordinary undertakings, that seemed impossible of accomplishment, have been successfully carried out. Enthusiasm makes weak men strong, and timid women courageous. Almost all the great works of art have been produced when the artist was intoxicated with a passion for beauty and form, which would not let him rest until his thought was expressed in marble or on canvas.

A recent writer has said: "Enthusiasm is life lit up and shining. It is the passion of the spirit pushing forward toward some noble activity. It is one of the most powerful forces that go to the making of a noble and heroic character."

In the Gallery of Fine Arts, in Paris, is a beautiful statue conceived by a sculptor who was so poor that he lived and worked in a small garret. When his clay model was nearly done, a heavy frost fell upon the city. He knew that if the water in the interstices of the clay should freeze, the beautiful lines would be distorted. So he wrapped his bedclothes around the clay image to preserve it from destruction. In the morning he was found dead; but his idea was saved, and other hands gave it enduring form in marble.

Another instance of rare consecration to a great enterprise is found in the work of the late Francis Parkman. While a student at Harvard, he determined to write the history of the French and English in North America. With a steadiness and devotion seldom equaled, he gave his life, his fortune, his all, to this one great object. Although he had ruined his health while among the Dakota Indians, collecting material for his history, and could not use his eyes more than five minutes at a time for fifty years, he did not swerve a hair's breadth from the high purpose formed in his youth, until he gave to the world the best history upon this subject ever written.

What a power there is in an enthusiastic adherence to an ideal! What are hardships, ridicule, persecution, toil, or sickness, to a soul throbbing with an overmastering purpose? Gladstone says that "what is really wanted, is to light up the spirit that is within a boy." In some sense, and in some degree, there is in every boy the material for doing good work in the world; not only in those who are brilliant and quick, but even in those who are stolid and dull.

A real enthusiasm makes men happy, keeps them fresh, hopeful, joyous. Life never stagnates with them. They always keep sweet, anticipate a "good time coming," and help to make it come.

Enthusiasm has been well called the "lever of the world"; for it sets in motion, if it does not control, the grandest revolutions! Its influence is immense. History bears frequent record of its contagiousness, showing how vast multitudes have been roused into emotion by the enthusiasm of one man; as was the case when the crowd of knights, and squires, and men-at-arms, and quiet peasants, entered, at the bidding of St. Bernard, upon the great Crusade.

The simple, innocent Maid of Orleans,—with her sacred sword, her consecrated banner, and her belief in her great mission,—sent a thrill of enthusiasm through the whole French army such as neither king nor statesman could produce. Her zeal carried everything before it.

Enthusiasm makes men strong. It wakes them up, brings out their latent powers, keeps up incessant action, impels to tasks requiring strength, and then carries them to completion. Many are born to be giants, yet, from lack of enthusiasm, few grow above common men. They need to be set on fire by some eager impulse, inspired by some grand resolve, and they would then quickly rise head and shoulders above their fellows.

Enthusiasm is the element of success in everything. It is the light that leads, and the strength that lifts men on and up in the great struggles of scientific pursuits and of professional labors. It robs endurance of difficulty, and makes a pleasure of duty.

Enthusiasm gives to man a power that is irresistible. It is that secret and harmonious spirit which hovers over the production of genius, throwing the reader of a book, or the spectator of a statue, into the presence of those with whom these works have originated. A great work always leaves us in a state of lofty contemplation, if we are in sympathy with it.

The most irresistible charm of youth is its bubbling enthusiasm. The youth who comes fully under its control sees no darkness ahead. He forgets that there is such a thing as failure in the world, and believes that mankind has been waiting all these centuries for him to come and be the liberator of truth and energy and beauty.

The boy Bach copied whole books of musical studies by moonlight, for want of a candle churlishly denied. Nor was he disheartened when these copies were taken from him. The boy painter West, began his work in a garret, and cut hairs from the tail of the family cat for bristles to make his brushes. Gerster, an unknown Hungarian singer, made fame and fortune sure the first night she appeared in opera. Her enthusiasm almost mesmerized her auditors. In less than a week she had become popular and independent. Her soul was smitten with a passion for growth, and all the powers of heart and mind were devoted to self-improvement.

Enthusiasm is purified and ennobled by self-denial. As the traveler, who would ascend a lofty mountain summit, to enjoy the sunset there, leaves the quiet of the lowly vale, and climbs the difficult path, so the true enthusiast, in his aspiration after the highest good, allows himself to be stopped by no wish for wealth and pleasure, and every step he takes forward is connected with self-denial, but is a step nearer to success.

THOMAS A. EDISON.

If one were to ask what individual best typifies the industrial progress of this nation, it would be easy to answer, Thomas Alva Edison. Looking at him as a newspaper boy, at the age of fifteen, one would hardly have been led to predict that this young fellow would be responsible for the industrial transformation of this continent.

At that early age he had already begun to dabble in chemistry, and had fitted up a small traveling laboratory. One day, as he was performing an experiment, the train rounded a curve and the bottles of chemicals were dashed to the floor. There followed a series of unearthly odors and unnatural complications. The conductor, who had suffered long and patiently, now ejected the youthful enthusiast; and, it is said, accompanied the expulsion with a resounding box upon the ear. This did not dampen Edison's ardor, in the least. He passed through one dramatic situation after another, mastering each and all; but his advancement was due to patient, persevering work.

Not long ago a reporter asked him if he had regular hours for work. "Oh!" he answered, "I do not work hard now. I come to the laboratory about eight o'clock every day, and go home to tea at six; and then I study and work on some problem until eleven, which is my hour for bed."

When it was suggested that fourteen or fifteen hours' work per day could scarcely be called loafing, he replied, "Well, for fifteen years I have worked on an average twenty hours a day." Nothing but a rare devotion to an interesting subject could keep any man so diligently employed. So enthusiastically did he pursue his researches, that, when he had once started to solve a difficult problem, he has been known to work at it for sixty consecutive hours.

In describing his Boston experiences, Edison relates that he bought Faraday's works on electricity, and beginning to read them at three o'clock in the morning, continued until his room-mate arose, when they started on their long walk for breakfast. Breakfast, however, was of small account in Edison's mind compared with his love for Faraday; and he suddenly remarked to his friend, "Adams, I have so much to do, and life is so short, that I must hustle;" and with that he started off on a dead run for the boarding-house.

Edison has shown that he cares nothing for money, and has no particular enthusiasm for fame. "What makes you work so hard?" asked a friend. "I like it," he answered, after a moment's puzzled expression; and then repeated several times, "I like it. I do not know any other reason. You know how some people like to collect stamps. Anything I have begun is always on my mind, and I am not easy while away from it until it is finished."

Electrical science is still in its infancy, but the enthusiasm of Edison has done much for its advancement. The subject indeed is a fascinating one, and Edison's devotion to it, and the discoveries and practical applications he has made in his researches, have placed him in the front rank of America's greatest inventors.

[Footnote: See Review of Reviews, Vol. XVIII., and articles in encyclopedias.]

XXII.

COURAGE.

MEMORY GEMS.

The best hearts are always the bravest.—Sterne

In noble souls, valor does not wait for years.—Corneille

Courage is always greatest when blended with meekness.—Earl Stanhope

A brave man hazards life, but not his conscience.—Schiller

A great deal of talent is lost in the world for want of a little courage.—Sydney Smith

The definition of courage given by Webster is, "that quality of mind which enables men to encounter danger and difficulties with firmness or without fear or depression of spirits." We would rather say that courage does not consist in feeling no fear, but in conquering fear. Our meaning will perhaps be best made clear by the following illustrations:

Two French officers at Waterloo were advancing to charge a greatly superior force. One, observing that the other showed signs of fear, said "Sir, I believe you are frightened." "Yes, I am," was the reply; "and if you were half as much frightened, you would run away."

"That's a brave man," said Wellington, when he saw a soldier turn pale as he marched against a battery; "he knows his danger, and faces it."

Genuine courage is based on something more than animal strength; and this holds true always. Cowardly hearts are often encased in giant frames. Slender women often display astounding bravery.

The courageous man is a real helper in the work of the world's advancement. His influence is magnetic. He creates an epidemic of nobleness. Men follow him, even to the death.

"Our enemies are before us," exclaimed the Spartans at Thermopylae. "And we are before them," was the cool reply of Leonidas. "Deliver your arms," came the message from Xerxes. "Come and take them," was the answer Leonidas sent back. A Persian soldier said: "You will not be able to see the sun for flying javelins and arrows." "Then we will fight in the shade," replied a Lacedaemonian. What wonder that a handful of such men checked the march of the greatest host that ever trod the earth.

Don't be like Uriah Heep, begging everybody's pardon for taking the liberty of being in the world. There is nothing attractive in timidity, nothing lovable in fear. Both are deformities, and are repulsive. Manly courage is dignified and graceful.

The spirit of courage will transform the whole temper of your life. "The wise and active conquer difficulties by daring to attempt them. The lazy and the foolish shiver and sicken at the sight of trial and hazard, and create the very impossibility they fear."

Abraham Lincoln's boyhood was one long struggle with poverty, with little education, and no influential friends. When at last he had begun the practice of law, it required no little daring to cast his fortune with the weaker side in politics, and thus imperil what small reputation he had gained. Only the most sublime moral courage could have sustained him as President to hold his ground against hostile criticism and a long train of disaster, to issue the Emancipation Proclamation, to support Grant and Stanton against the clamor of the politicians and the press, and, through it all, to do what he believed to be right.

Did you ever read the fable of the magician and the mouse? It is worth reading in this connection:

A mouse that dwelt near the abode of a great magician, was kept in such constant fear of a cat, that the magician, taking pity on it, turned it into a cat itself. Immediately it began to suffer from its fear of a dog, so the magician turned it into a dog. Then it began to suffer from fear of a tiger. The magician therefore turned it into a tiger. Then it began to suffer from fear of hunters, and the magician said in disgust: "Be a mouse again. As you have only the heart of a mouse, it is impossible to help you by giving you the body of a nobler animal." The moral of the story you can gather for yourselves.

We have already said that many women have displayed courage of a very high order. Here is a case in point:

Charles V. of Spain passed through Thuringia in 1547, on his return to Swabia after the battle of Muehlburg. He wrote to Catherine, Countess Dowager of Schwartzburg, promising that her subjects should not be molested in their persons or property if they would supply the Spanish soldiers with provisions at a reasonable price. On approaching her residence, General Alva and Prince Henry of Brunswick, with his sons, invited themselves, by a messenger sent forward, to breakfast with the Countess, who had no choice but to ratify so delicate a request from the commander of an army. Just as the guests were seated at a generous repast, the Countess was called from the hall and told that the Spaniards were using violence and driving away the cattle of the peasants.

Quietly arming all her retinue, she bolted and barred all the gates and doors of the castle, and returned to the banquet to complain of the breach of faith.

General Alva told her that such was the custom of war, adding that such trifling disorders were not to be heeded. "That we shall presently see," said Catherine; "my poor subjects must have their own again, or, as God lives, prince's blood for oxen's blood!" The doors were opened, and armed men took the place of the waiters behind the chairs of the guests. Henry changed color; then, as the best way out of a bad scrape, laughed loudly, and ended by praising the splendid acting of his hostess, and promising that Alva should order the cattle restored at once. Not until a courier returned, saying that the order had been obeyed, and all damages settled satisfactorily, did the armed waiters leave. The Countess then thanked her guests for the honor they had done her castle, and they retired with protestations of their distinguished consideration.

There is a form of moral courage which bears most directly upon ourselves. It is seen in the career of William H. Seward, who was given a thousand dollars by his father to go to college with, and told that this was all he was to have. The son returned home at the end of his freshman year with extravagant habits and no money. His father refused to give him more, and told him he could not stay at home. When the youth found the props all taken out from under him, and that he must now sink or swim, he left home moneyless, returned to college, graduated at the head of his class, studied law, was elected governor of New York, and became Lincoln's great Secretary of State during the Civil War.

Genuine courage is neither rash, vain, nor selfish. It sometimes leadsus to appear cowardly; and cowardice sometimes puts on the guise of boldness. We need to know the individual and the circumstances to judge correctly as to whether courage is of the true order. We should all discourage the tendency to exalt brute force and mere muscle to high admiration; and enforce the power of mind, ideas, and lofty ambition. The noblest phase of courage and heroism is in the submission of this might to the laws of right and helpfulness.

RICHARD PEARSON HOBSON.

There is no better modern illustration of courage than that thrilling exploit of Lieutenant Hobson in taking the Merrimac into the harbor of Santiago.

While the Spanish fleet, under Admiral Cervera, lay blockaded in Santiago Bay, the idea was conceived of making the blockade doubly safe by sinking the coal-ship Merrimac across the narrow channel. To carry out this plan cool-headed, heroic men were needed, who would be willing to take their lives in their hands, for the good of their country's cause. To accomplish the object, the vessel must be taken into a harbor full of mines, under the fire of three shore batteries, supported by a powerful Spanish fleet and two regiments of soldiers. The honor of carrying out this bold scheme was given to young Hobson, by whom the plan had been mainly outlined.

He was a young man from Alabama, twenty-seven years of age, a graduate of the Naval Academy in the class of 1889, being the youngest member, and standing at the head of his class. He had already shown himself to be a gentleman, a student, and an adept in practical affairs. Now he was to prove that he was a hero.

Here came to him, in the ordinary course of duty, the opportunity for which he had prepared himself; and the courage with which he carried it out made for him a name which will always be remembered in the annals of naval warfare.

Out of the hundreds who volunteered to assist him in this perilous undertaking, six men were selected. At an early hour in the morning the gallant crew set out. Every vessel in the American fleet was on the alert: every man's nerves were at the highest tension over the success of the project and the fate of Hobson and his comrades. Thousands of anxious eyes peered through the darkness as they watched the old collier disappear into the harbor.

Suddenly the scene changed. Sheets of fire flashed from Morro Castle and the other batteries along the shore. It seemed impossible for human life to exist in that deadly and concentrated fire. In the downpour of shot and shell the Merrimac's rudder was blown away and her stern anchor cut loose. The electric batteries were damaged to such an extent that only part of the torpedoes could be exploded. The result was that instead of sinking where intended, the vessel drifted with the tide past the narrow neck. The Merrimac sank but did not completely block up the channel.

The enemy's fire was so incessant and sweeping that it was impossible for the crew to reach the life-raft which they had in tow; so Hobson and his men lay flat on deck and waited for the ship to sink. It was a terrible waiting while every great gun and Mauser rifle was pouring its deadly fire upon the ship. At last the end came. The ship sank beneath the waves, and, through the whirlpool of rushing water, the men rose to the surface and climbed upon their raft. Clinging to this, with their faces only out of water they waited for daylight, and then gave themselves up as prisoners to the Spaniards.

In the afternoon, Admiral Cervera sent an officer, under a flag of truce, to Admiral Sampson, telling him of their safety, and adding: "Daring like theirs makes the bitterest enemies proud that their fellow-men can be so brave."

[Footnote: See Review of Reviews, Vol. XVIII., and Draper's "The Rescue of Cuba" and other war stories recently published.]

XXIII.

SELF-HELP.

MEMORY GEMS.

Our remedies oft in ourselves do lie, which we ascribe to Heaven.
—Shakespeare

Be sure, my son, and remember that the best men always make themselves.
—Patrick Henry.

God gives every bird its food, but he does not throw it into the nest.
—J. G. Holland

Every person has two educations, one which he receives from others, and one, more important, which he gives himself.—Gibbon

In battle or business, whatever the game,
In law, or in love it is ever the same:
In the struggle for power, or the scramble for pelf,
Let this be your motto, "Rely on yourself."—J. G. Saxe

History and biography unite in teaching that circumstances have rarely favored great men. They have fought their way to triumph over the road of difficulty and through all sorts of opposition. Boys of lowly origin have made many of the greatest discoveries, are presidents of our banks, of our colleges, of our universities. Our poor boys and girls have written many of our greatest books, and have filled the highest places as teachers and journalists. Ask almost any great man in our large cities where he was born, and he will tell you it was on a farm or in a small country village. Nearly all the great capitalists of the city came from the country.

Frederick Douglass, America's most representative colored man, was born a slave, reared in bondage, liberated by his own exertions, educated and advanced by sheer pluck and perseverance, to distinguished positions in the service of his country, and to a high place in the respect and esteem of the whole world.

Chauncey Jerome, the inventor of machine-made clocks, started with twoothers on a tour through New Jersey, they to sell the clocks, and he to make cases for them. On his way to New York he went through New Haven, Connecticut, in a lumber wagon, eating bread and cheese. He afterward lived in a fine mansion in that city, and stood very high among its people.

Men who have been bolstered up all their lives are seldom good for anything in a crisis. When misfortune comes, they look around for somebody to lean upon. If the prop is not there down they go. Once down, they are helpless as capsized turtles. Many a boy has succeeded beyond all his expectations simply because all props were knocked out from under him and he was obliged to stand upon his own feet. "Poverty is uncomfortable, as I can testify," said James A. Garfield; "but nine times out of ten the best thing that can happen to a young man is to be tossed overboard and compelled to sink or swim for himself. In all my acquaintance I have never known a man to be drowned who was worth the saving."

What is put into the first of life is put into the whole of life. The great London preacher, Mr. Spurgeon, once said "Out of a church of twenty-seven hundred members, I have never had to exclude a single one who was received while a child;" and in other respects it is equally true that our earliest impressions and habits most powerfully influence our later life.

Washington, at thirteen, copied into his commonplace book one hundred and ten maxims of civility and good behavior, and was most careful in the formation of all his habits. Franklin, too, devised a plan of self-improvement and character-building. No doubt the noble characters of these two men, almost superhuman in their excellence, are the natural result of their early care and earnest striving toward perfection.

But the opposite truth needs to be quite as fully considered. "Many men of genius have written worse scrawls than I do," said a boy at Eugby, when his teacher remonstrated with him for his bad penmanship; "it is not worth while to worry about so trivial a fault." Ten years later, when he had become an officer in the Crimea, his illegible copy of an order caused the loss of many brave men.

The insidious growth of the power of habit is well illustrated by the old fable which says that one of the Fates spun filaments so fine that they were invisible, and then became a victim of her own cunning; for she was bound to the spot by these very threads.

There is also a story of a Grecian flute-player who charged double fees for pupils who had been taught by inferior masters, on the ground that it was much harder to undo bad habits than to form good ones.

"Conduct," says Matthew Arnold, "is three fourths of life;" but conduct has its source in character. Right conduct in life is to be secured by the formation of right character in youth. The prime element in character, as related to conduct, is the power of self-directions and hence the supreme aim of school discipline is to prepare the young to be self-governing men and women.

An easy and luxurious existence does not train men to effort or encounter with difficulty; nor does it awaken that consciousness of power which is so necessary for energetic and effective action in life. Indeed, so far from poverty being a misfortune, it may, by vigorous self-help, be converted into a blessing.

A young man stood listlessly watching some anglers on a bridge. He was poor and dejected. At length, approaching a basket filled with fish, he sighed, "If now I had these I would be happy. I could sell them and buy food and lodging." "I will give you just as many and just as good," said the owner, who chanced to overhear his words, "if you will do me a trifling favor." "And what is that?" asked the other. "Only to tend this line till I come back; I wish to go on a short errand." The proposal was gladly accepted. The old man was gone so long that the young man began to get impatient. Meanwhile the fish snapped greedily at the hook, and he lost all his depression in the excitement of pulling them in. When the owner returned he had caught a large number. Counting out from them as many as were in the basket, and presenting them to the youth, the old fisherman said, "I fulfill my promise from the fish you have caught, to teach you whenever you see others earning what you need, to waste no time in foolish wishing, but cast a line for yourself."

After a stained-glass window had been constructed for a great European cathedral, an artist picked up the discarded fragments and made one of the most exquisite windows in Europe for another cathedral. So one boy will pick up a splendid education out of the odds and ends of time which others carelessly throw away, or he will gain a fortune by saving what others waste.

There is an English fable that is worthy of special attention. The story is as follows:

Some larks had a nest in a field of grain. One evening the old larks coming home found the young ones in great terror. "We must leave our nest at once," they cried. Then they related how they had heard the farmer say that he must get his neighbors to come the next day and help him reap his field. "Oh!" cried the old birds, "if that is all, we may rest quietly in our nest." The next evening the young birds were found again in a state of terror. The farmer, it seems, was very angry because his neighbors had not come, and had said that he should get his relatives to come the next day and help him. The old birds took the news easily, and said there was nothing to fear yet. The next evening the young birds were quite cheerful. "Have you heard nothing to-day?" asked the old ones. "Nothing important," answered the young. "It is only that the farmer was angry because his relatives also failed him, and he said to his sons, 'Since neither our neighbors nor our relations will help us, we must take hold to-morrow and do it ourselves!'" The old birds were excited this time. They said, "We must leave our nest to-night. When a man decides to do a thing for himself, and to do it at once, you may be pretty sure that it will be done."

If you have anything to do, do it yourself; for that is both the surest and the safest way to permanent success.

STEPHEN GIRAD.

We present by way of special illustration, a few incidents from the career of Stephen Girard.

A sloop was seen one morning off the mouth of Delaware Bay, floating the flag of France and a signal of distress. Girard, then quite a young man, was captain of this sloop, and was on his way to a Canadian port with freight from New Orleans. An American skipper, seeing his distress, went to his aid, but told him the American war had broken out, and that the British cruisers were all along the American coast, and would seize his vessel. He told him his only chance was to make a push for Philadelphia. Girard did not know the way, and was short of money. The skipper loaned him five dollars to get the service of a pilot who demanded his money in advance; and his sloop passed into the Delaware just in time to avoid capture by a British war vessel. He sold the sloop and cargo in Philadelphia, and began business on the capital. Being a foreigner, unable to speak English, with a repulsive face, and blind in one eye, it was hard for him to get a start. But he was not the man to give up.

There seemed to be nothing he would not do for money. He bought and sold anything, from groceries to old junk. Everything he touched prospered. In 1780, he resumed the New Orleans and San Domingo trade, in which he had been engaged at the breaking out of the War of the Revolution, and in one year cleared nearly fifty thousand dollars.

Everybody, especially his jealous brother merchants, attributed his great success to his luck. While, undoubtedly, he was fortunate in happening to be at the right place at the right time, yet he was precision, method, accuracy, energy itself. He left nothing to chance. His plans and schemes were worked out with mathematical care. His letters, written to his captains in foreign ports, laying out their routes and giving detailed instruction from which they were never allowed to deviate under any circumstances, are models of foresight and systematic planning.

Girard never lost a ship; and many times, what brought financial ruin to many others, as the War of 1812, only increased his wealth. What seemed luck with him was only good judgment and promptness in seizing opportunities, and the greatest care and zeal in personal attention to all the details of his business and the management of his own affairs.

[Footnote: See Simpson's "Life of Stephen Girard" (Phila. 1832), and H. W. Arey's "Girard College and its Founder" (1860).]

XXIV.

HUMILITY.

MEMORY GEMS.

Humility is the true cure for many a needless heartache.—A. Montague

It is easy to look down on others; to look down on ourselves is the difficulty.—Lord Peterborough

Humility is a divine veil which covers our good deeds, and hides them from our eyes.—St. John Climacas

Humility is the root, mother, nurse, foundation, and bond of all virtue.—Chrysostom

Modest humility is beauty's crown; for the beautiful is a hidden thing, and shrinks from its own power.—Schiller

We pass now from the strong and active virtue of self-help, to the gentle and passive virtue of humility. In doing so, we quickly discover that it requires a sound moral judgment to strike the right balance between humility and self-reliance, and between meekness and self-respect. The true man is both meek and self-reliant, humble and yet by no means incapable of self-assertion. The really strong man is the most thoroughly gentle of men, and the genuinely self-confident man is the one who is most truly humble in his regard for the rights and interests of others.

We have great need of this particular grace, and we ought to study its relation to our life in general; for we should often have reason to be ashamed of our most brilliant actions if the world could see the motives from which they spring.

Humility has been well defined as "a simple and lowly estimation of one's self." When practically thought of, it is mostly looked upon in a negative light, and considered as the absence of, or opposite to, pride.

The general line of human thinking rather tends in the opposite direction; but experience teaches that if we wish to be great, we shall do well to begin by being little. If we desire to construct a strong and noble character, we must not forget that the greatest lives have always rested on foundations of humility. The higher your structure is to be, the deeper must be its foundation.

Humility does not consist in a disposition falsely to underrate ourselves, "but in being willing to waive our rights, and descend to a lower place than is our due; in being ready to admit our liability to error, and in freely owning our faults when conscious of having been wrong; and, in short, in not being over-careful of our own dignity."

This virtue is the friend of intellect instead of its enemy, because humility is both a moral instinct which seeks truth, and a moral instrument for attaining truth. It leads us to base our knowledge on truth; it also leads us truthfully to recognize the real measure of our capacity.

All really great men have been humble men in spirit and temper. Such was Lincoln; such was Washington. Izaac Walton relates how George Herbert helped a poor man whose horse had fallen under his load, laying off his coat for that purpose, aiding him to unload, and then again to load his cart. When his friends rebuked Herbert for this service he said that "the thought of what he had done would prove music to him at midnight, for he felt bound, so far as was in his power, to practice that for which he prayed."

An instance often cited, but always beautiful, is that of Sir Philip Sidney when mortally wounded at Zutphen as described by an old writer: "Being thirsty with an excess of bleeding, he called for drink, which was presently brought him; but as he was putting the bottle to his mouth, he saw a poor soldier carried along, casting up his eyes at the bottle; which Sir Philip perceiving, took it from his lips before he drank, and delivered it to the poor man with these words: 'Thy necessity is yet greater than mine.'" It mattered nothing to Sir Philip that he was an officer and therefore of higher standing than the poor private. He humbled himself and did a kindly action, and his noble deed will never be forgotten.

Humility is not lack of courage; it is not the poverty of spirit which shrinks from encounter. So far from destroying moral force, it protects and strengthens it; it sternly represses the little vanities through which strength of character evaporates and is lost. It is a noble trait in peasant or in prince, in the cottage of the workman or in the mansion of the millionaire.

Trajan, the Roman emperor, has set us an example of condescension and affability. He was equal, indeed, to the greatest generals of antiquity; but the sounding titles bestowed upon him by his admirers did not elate him. All the oldest soldiers he knew by name. He conversed with them with the greatest familiarity, and never retired to his tent before he had visited the camps. He refused the statues which the flattery of friends wished to erect to him, and he ridiculed the follies of an enlightened nation that could pay adoration to cold inanimate pieces of marble. His public entry into Rome gained him the hearts of the people; for he appeared on foot, and showed himself an enemy to parade and ostentatious equipage. His wish to listen to the just complaints of his subjects, caused his royal abode to be called "the public palace"; and his people learned to love him as greatly as they admired him.

True humility is not cowardly, cringing, or abjectly weak. It is strength putting itself by the side of weakness through sympathy, and not weakness abasing itself in the presence of that which it pretends is greater than itself. The humble man is the man who feels his own imperfection, and therefore does not condemn another. The truly humble say very little about their humility, except in rare moments of emotion, but live and labor in quietness for the promotion of the public good.

Sincerity and lowliness of spirit have been often commended, as when the Pythian Apollo rebuked the pompous sacrifice offered at his shrine by a rich Magnesian, and said that he preferred the simple cake and frankincense of a pious Achaean which was offered in humbleness of heart.

Do not allow yourselves to be deceived by false appearances, but lay to heart the story of the farmer who went with his son into a wheatfield to see if it was ready for the harvest. "See, father," exclaimed the boy, "how straight these stems hold up their heads! They must be the best ones. These that hang their heads down cannot be good for much." The farmer plucked a stalk of each kind, and said, "See here, foolish child! This stalk that stood so straight is light-headed, and almost good for nothing; while this that hung its head so modestly is full of the most beautiful grain."

"Humility is like the violet which grows low, and covers itself with its own leaves, and yet of all flowers, yields the most delicious and fragrant smell."

This virtue is not to be confounded with mean-spiritedness, or that abject state of feeling which permits a man to surrender the rights of his character to any one who chooses to infringe upon them. While it thinks little of personal considerations, it thinks the more of character and principle. It is really a powerful aid to progress. When we realize how little we know, we shall earnestly strive to know more; when we feel how imperfect is our character, we shall make earnest efforts after improvement.

PHILLIPS BROOKS.

Phillips Brooks may certainly be ranked among the greatest men of the present generation. He was physically and mentally strong; possessed of a great personality that compelled him to self-assertion; and was self-reliant in a degree attained by but few men of his time. He followed his own convictions, in the face of much opposition, bravely and unflinchingly. But with all his greatness and self-confidence, he was gentle, tolerant, sympathetic, and thoroughly appreciative of the rights of others. He made himself felt everywhere; yet he never indulged in controversy, and never struck back when criticised. He used his strength for the good of the weak; he asserted himself in a meek and humble spirit.

The story of his caring for the children of a poor woman, in the slums of Boston while she went out for needed recreation, shows that in the greatness of his manhood he could stoop to the lowliest tasks; while his unbounded love for children, kept him bright and young down to the very close of his honored career.

To understand this side of his character, we recommend you to read his "Letters to Children," of which the following, written to his niece, is an excellent example:

"VENICE, August 13, 1882.

"DEAR GERTIE:—When the little children in Venice want to take a bath, they just go down to the front steps of the house and jump off and swim about in the street. Yesterday I saw a nurse standing on the front steps, holding one end of a string, and the other end was tied to a little fellow who was swimming up the street. When he went too far, the nurse pulled in the string, and got her baby home again. Then I met another youngster, swimming in the street, whose mother had tied him to a post by the side of the door, so that when he tried to swim away to see another boy who was tied to another door-post up the street, he couldn't, and they had to sing out to one another over the water. Is not this a queer city? You are always in danger of running over some of the people and drowning them, for you go about in a boat instead of a carriage, and use an oar instead of a horse. But it is ever so pretty, and the people, especially the children, are very bright and gay and handsome.

"When you are sitting in your room at night, you hear some music under your window, and look out, and there is a boat with a man with a fiddle, and a woman with a voice, and they are serenading you. To be sure, they want some money when they are done, for everybody begs here; but they do it very prettily and are full of fun.

"Tell Susie I did not see the queen this time. She was out of town. But ever so many noblemen and princes have sent to know how Toody was, and how she looked, and I have sent them all her love.

"There must be lots of pleasant things to do at Andover, and I think you must have had a beautiful summer there. Pretty soon now you will go back to Boston. Do go into my house when you get there and see if the doll and her baby are well and happy, but do not carry them off; and make the music-box play a tune, and remember your affectionate uncle, PHILLIPS."

[Footnote: No really good life of Phillips Brooks has yet been published; but consult his "Letters of Travel," and the numerous articles in the best magazines.]

XXV.

FAITHFULNESS.

MEMORY GEMS.

Faithfulness is the soul of goodness.—J. S. White

That which we love most in men and women is faithfulness.—S. Brooke

It is the fidelity in the daily drill which turns the raw recruit into the accomplished soldier.—W. M. Punshon

The secret of success in life is for a man to be faithful to all his duties and obligations.—Disraeli

The truest test of civilization is not the census, nor the size of cities, nor the crops; but the kind of men the country turns out.—Emerson

Faithfulness is just as possible to boys and girls as to men and women. To be faithful is to be true to our own convictions,—never acting without or against them,—and true to our professions,—never breaking promises, or swerving from engagements.

Exactly what we mean will readily be seen in the following incident: When Blucher was hastening over bad roads to help Wellington at Waterloo, his troops faltered. "It can't be done," said they. "It *must* be done," was his reply. "I have promised to be there—*promised*, do you hear? You wouldn't have me break my word!" It was done, as we all know; and the result of his faithfulness was a great victory for Wellington, and the complete overthrow of Napoleon.

Faithfulness in the daily routine of school work has laid the foundation of many a noble character. There is no one thing which will sooner wreck a young man, and utterly ruin his future prospects, than the reputation of being lazy and shiftless.

Mr. Ruskin, speaking of the importance of faithfulness among the young people of England, said, "Could I give the youth of this country but one word of advice it would be this: *Let no moment pass until you have extracted from it every possibility. Watch every grain in the hourglass.*"

Sir Walter Scott, writing to his son at school, says: "I cannot too much impress upon your mind that faithfulness is a condition imposed on us in every station of life; there is nothing worth having that can be had without it. As for knowledge, it can no more be planted in the human mind without labor than a field of wheat can be produced without the previous use of the plow. If we neglect our spring, our summer will be useless and contemptible, our harvest will be chaff, and the winter of our old age unrespected and desolate."

It will be seen, therefore, that all young persons should endeavor to make each day stand for something. Neither heaven nor earth has any place for the drone; he is a libel on his species. No glamour of wealth or social prestige can hide his essential ugliness. It is better to carry a hod, or wield a shovel, in an honest endeavor to be of some use to humanity, than to be nursed in luxury and be a parasite.

The emptiness and misery sometimes found in idle high life is illustrated by the following letter, written by a French countess to the absent count:

"DEAR HUSBAND:—Not knowing what else to do I will write to you. Not knowing what to say, I will now close. Wearily yours, COUNTESS DE R."

Of course we must admit that there is variety in the distribution of human talents; and yet no one of us is incompletely furnished. Each one has to be faithful only according to the measure of his trust, and is not expected to make disproportionate gains. Some men are especially fortunate both in opportunities and in resources, while to others, chances of advancement come but seldom; but the man of few opportunities may be just as faithful as the man who has many.

If you would be accounted faithful, you must do little things as if they were great, and great things as if they were little and easy. That is the true road to success; and your place or station in life has very little to do with it.

Calais is a pleasant seaport town of France, situated on the Straits of Dover. Large numbers of travelers from England to France, and from France to England, pass through this beautiful town. Near the center of it is a lighthouse, one hundred and eighteen feet high, on which is placed a revolving light that can be seen by vessels twenty miles out at sea.

At one time some gentlemen were visiting the tower upon which the light is placed, when the watchman who has charge of the burners commenced praising their brilliancy. One of the gentlemen then said to him, "What if one of the lights should chance to go out?" "Impossible!" replied the watchman, with amazement at the bare thought of such neglect of duty. "Sir," said he, pointing to the ocean, "yonder, where nothing can be seen, there are ships going to every part of the world. If to-night one of my burners were out, within six months would come a letter—from India, perhaps from the islands of the Pacific Ocean, perhaps from some place I never heard of—saying that on such a night, at such an hour, the light of Calais burned dim; the watchman neglected his post, and vessels were in danger. Ah, sir, sometimes on dark nights, in the stormy weather, I look out at sea, and I feel as if the eyes of the whole world were looking at my light! My light go out! Calais's burners grow dim! No, never!"

Exactly the opposite of this is seen in the incident which follows:

A few years ago, the keeper of a life-saving station on the Atlantic coast found that his supply of powder had given out. The nearest village was two or three miles distant, and the weather was inclement. He concluded that it "was not worth while to go so far for such a trifle." That night a vessel was wrecked within sight of the station. A line could have been given to the crew if he had been able to use the mortar; but he had no powder. He saw the drowning men perish one by one, knowing that he alone was to blame. A few days afterward he was justly dismissed from the service.

Faithfulness must especially take into account the feelings and expectations we have raised in other minds. In this matter we cannot be too careful. It is said of Lord Chatham that he once promised his son that he should be present at the pulling down of a garden wall. The wall was, however, taken down during his absence, through forgetfulness; but, feeling the importance of his word being held sacred, Lord Chatham ordered the workman to rebuild it, that his son might witness its destruction according to his father's promise.

Loyalty is also a form of faithfulness. It is patriotism in practice. Only the patriotic citizen is loyal to his country. The absence of this sentiment, in times of national peril, exposes one to indecision and cowardice, if not to treason. Hence its great value and beauty. It is indispensable to good citizenship; indeed there is no true manhood and womanhood without it. It is involved in the American idea of republican institutions. It is loyalty alone which makes it possible for our country to continue on its course from year to year.

This form of faithfulness is just now commanding attention throughout our land. The national flag is flung to the breeze over our schoolhouses, that American youth may not forget their allegiance to the government it represents. The stars and stripes floating over the temples of knowledge, wherein our youth are being trained for usefulness and honor, is worth far more to us than we realize; and we should always be ready to hail it with joyous songs and cheers.

CYRUS W. FIELD.

One of the greatest enterprises of modern times, was the laying of the first Atlantic cable. Cyrus W. Field became impressed with the feasibility of this project. He induced capitalists to put their money into it; and then plunged into the work with all the force of his being. The faithfulness with which he performed his task gained for him the united praise of two continents.

By hard work he secured aid for his company from the British government; but in Congress he encountered such bitter opposition from a powerful lobby that his measure had a majority of only one in the senate.

The cable was loaded upon the Agamemnon, the flagship of the British fleet at Sebastopol, and upon the Niagara, a magnificent new frigate of the United States navy; but, when five miles of cable had been paid out, it caught in the machinery and parted. On the second trial, when two hundred miles at sea, the electric current was suddenly lost, and men paced the decks nervously and sadly, as if in the presence of death. Just as Mr. Field was about to give the order to cut the cable, the current returned as quickly and mysteriously as it had disappeared. The following night, when the ship was moving but four miles an hour and the cable running out at the rate of six miles, the brakes were applied too suddenly just as the steamer gave a heavy lurch, and the cable broke and sank to the bottom of the sea.

Directors were disheartened, the public skeptical, capitalists were shy, and, but for the faith of Mr. Field, who worked day and night, almost without food or sleep, the whole project would have been abandoned.

A third attempt also resulted in failure, but not discouraged by all these difficulties, Mr. Field went to work with a will, organized a new company, and made a new cable far superior to anything before used; and, on July 13, 1866, was begun the trial which ended with the following message sent to New York:

"HEART'S CONTENT, July 27.

"We arrived here at nine o'clock this morning. All well. Thank God! the cable is laid and is in perfect working order. CYRUS W. FIELD."

Such, in brief, is the story of the faithful performance of a seemingly impossible task. It was a long, hard struggle, covering nearly thirteen years of anxious watching and ceaseless toil. But the name and fame of Cyrus W. Field will long be cherished and remembered by a grateful people.

[Footnote: See Appleton's "Cyclopedia of American Biography," Vol. II., pp. 448, 449, and Johnson's "Universal Cyclopedia," Vol. III., p. 351.]

XXVI.

THE SECOND TEANSITION PERIOD.

MEMORY GEMS.

It is the pushing fellows who get well to the front.—William Black

The tricky, underhanded individual pays higher for all he gets.
—W. M. Thackeray

A man ought to be something more than the son of his father.
—J. Staples White

Honor and shame from no condition rise;
Act well your part, there all the honor lies.—Pope

The darkest hour in the life of any young man is when he sits down to study how to get money without honestly earning it.—Horace Greeley

If we have seen that the first transition period in life is that which marks the passing of the child into the youth, then we may safely speak of the second transition period as that which marks the passing of the youth into the man.

Usually there is involved in this change the leaving of the parental home; the selecting of a business or profession; and, sometimes, the establishment of a new home, and the assuming of the cares of family life. It is, therefore, of importance that we should guard all the several interests of this period with more than ordinary care, and especially that we should acquaint ourselves with those facts and principles which have successfully guided others through a similar experience.

First of all we must make a careful study of our possibilities. Young men are constantly worrying lest they be failures and nonentities. Every man will count for all he is worth. There is as steady and constant a ratio between what a man is, and what he can accomplish, as there is between what a ton of dynamite is, and what it can accomplish. There is as much a science of success as there is a science of mathematics. A great deal depends on the matter of laying in supplies, accumulating primary stuff. A man is never too young to have that fact put before him, and never too old to have it rehearsed. He will understand and appreciate the truth of it before he gets through life; and it is a great pity for him not to have, at least, a little appreciation of it near the beginning, so as to frame his initial years in accordance with it.

Let, therefore, nothing escape your observation—deem nothing below your notice. Dive into all depths, and explore all hidden recesses that will render you a master of every department of any business or profession you may engage in. The man who can render himself generally useful has always a better chance of getting on in the world. Whatever you thoroughly acquire will be a source of satisfaction and profit to you throughout your future life. It will save you many an anxious hour by day, and many a restless one by night. Remember that the whole is made up of parts, and that the parts must be well understood before you can master the whole. You will never be able to manage your business successfully without a thorough knowledge of it in all its details. Resolve, therefore, at the very commencement of your career, to acquire such knowledge.

Young people sometimes say, "I shall never get an opportunity of showing what is in me, for every business is now so crowded." Shakespeare has answered this when he said, "There is a tide in the affairs of men, which taken at the flood, leads on to fortune." As a matter of fact opportunities come to all, but all are not ready for them when they come. Successful men are those who prepare themselves for all emergencies, and take advantage of the occasion when the favorable time comes.

A good many young men excuse themselves from ever becoming anything, or doing anything, by the fact that they always live where it is low tide. Perhaps that is because it is always low tide where they live. At any rate, the more we learn of the history of the men who have succeeded, the more apparent it becomes that if they were born in low water, they patched up their tattered circumstances, and beat out to sea on a tide of their own making.

If you would be a success in the business world, then you must master everything that you lay your hands upon. Bear in mind that this is your own interest, as well as your duty toward your employer. Think nothing below your attention; do not be afraid of drudgery. Investigate all, comprehend all, grasp all, and master all. Business, like an ingenious piece of machinery, is made up of many complicated parts. Analyze it, therefore, thoroughly search all its parts, and know for yourself how they are put together.

You may cherish the hope that you will one day be an employer yourself. It would be very desirable if we could repose unlimited confidence in the words and acts of our fellow-men; but, unfortunately, the condition of the world is not as yet sufficiently advanced to enable us to do so. Where you will find one that you can trust, you will find many that need watching. If you should be unacquainted with some of your business details, you must trust to others, and may in consequence be deceived. A few months of careful attention to it at the commencement of your career will secure you against deception throughout the whole of your life as an employer.

Then you must also be careful to remember that dividends in life are not paid until the investment of personal effort has been made. Sowing still antedates reaping; and the amount sowed determines pretty closely the size of the harvest. Whether it be young men or wheat fields the interest can be depended upon to keep up with the capital, and empty barns in October are the logical consequence of empty furrows in spring. The young man may as well understand that there are no gratuities in this life, and that success is never reached "across lots."

Success means, all the way through to the finish, a victory over difficulties; and if the young aspirant lacks the grit to face and down the difficulty that happens to confront him at the start, there is little reason to expect that his valor will show to any better advantage in his encounter with enemies that get in his way later.

Young men are apt to imitate each other. Let your conduct be such as to bear imitation; otherwise you will lead those who are younger than you to form injurious habits, and be the means of leading them away from the path of duty. It is an obligation you owe your seniors. In the discharge of their duties they will have to depend upon you to a certain extent; and if your part is not properly performed, the whole system must unavoidably suffer derangement.

If the mind is temperate in feeling, deliberate in choosing, and robust in its willing, character becomes set and enduring. If, on the contrary, feeling is volatile, choice fickle, and the will flabby, one quality after another awakens momentary admiration and impulse; ideals succeed each other as the vanishing visions of a dream; life is passed in a state of perpetual inward contradiction; and failure, both for yourselves and for your imitators, is almost sure to follow.

No young man can remain long in this unsettled or transition state; but he must become *something*. You will therefore do well to be careful how you tread this probationary ground; for it is really the one great opportunity of your lives so far as concerns the formation of your general characters. Use it thoughtfully and well, and your manhood will be stronger, richer, and more helpful, all through your later years.

XXVII.

ORDER.

MEMORY GEMS.

Accuracy is the twin brother of honesty.—C. Simmons

Without method, little can be done to any good purpose.—Macaulay

A place for everything, and everything in its place.—Old Proverb

Order is the law of all intelligible existence.—Blackie

Order is the sanity of the mind, the health of the body, the peace of the city, and the security of the state.—Southey

The two words "order" and "method" are so closely akin to each other that it is quite difficult to separate them, even in the mind. "Order is heaven's first law," it is said; also, "Method consists in the right choice of means to an end." Here a distinction is made; but the two words taken together, cover the line of thought we now wish to follow.

Children nowadays do not learn to read as they once did. They go to kindergartens; but order is the rule even in such play-schools, and it is the one great reason why they succeed. All schools and colleges depend upon order for successful work.

"He who every morning plans the transactions of the day," says Victor Hugo, "and follows out that plan, carries a thread that will guide him through the labyrinth of the most busy life. The orderly arrangement of his time is like a ray of light which darts itself through all his occupations. But where no plan is laid, where the disposal of time is surrendered merely to the chance of incidents, all things lie huddled together in one chaos, which admits of neither distribution nor review."

There is no talent like method; and no accomplishment that man can possess, like perseverance. These two powers will usually overcome every obstacle; and there is no position which a young man may not hope to secure, when, guided by these principles, he sets out upon the great highway of life. In after years, the manners and habits of the man are not so readily adapted to any prescribed course to which they have been unaccustomed. But in youth habits of system, method, and industry, are as easily formed as others; and the benefits and enjoyments which result from them, are more than the wealth and honors which they always secure.

"Never study on speculation," says Waters; "all such study is vain. Form a plan, have an object; then work for it, learn all you can about it, and you will be sure to succeed. What I mean by studying on speculation, is that aimless learning of things because they may be useful at some time; which is like the conduct of the woman who bought at auction a brass door-plate with the name Thompson on it, thinking it might some day be of service."

Orderly boys and girls are fair scholars, firm friends, and good planners; they make few mistakes, and succeed pretty well in all they do. Order does not make a genius; but a genius without order is exasperating when he is a man, and is only pardoned for his want of order when he is a boy because he is expected to do better each day. Begin with orderly *habits*; next day try order in *thought*; and then will follow naturally order in *principles*.

"You would be the greatest man of your age, Grattan," said Curran, "if you would buy a few yards of red tape and tie up your bills and papers." Curran realized that methodical people are accurate as a rule, and successful.

The celebrated Nathaniel Emmons, whose learning made him famous through all New England, claimed that he could not work at all, unless order reigned about him. For more than fifty years the same chairs stood in the same places in his study; his hat hung on the same hook; the shovel stood on the north side of the open fireplace, and the tongs on the south side; and all his books and papers were so arranged that he claimed to be able to find any information he needed in three or four minutes.

The demand for perfection in the make-up of Wendell Phillips was wonderful. Every word must express the exact shade of his thought; every phrase must be of due length and cadence; every sentence must be perfectly balanced before it left his lips. Exact precision characterized his style. He was easily the first legal orator America has produced. The rhythmical fullness and poise of his periods are remarkable.

A. T. Stewart was extremely systematic and precise in all his transactions. Method ruled in every department of his store, and for every delinquency a penalty was rigidly enforced. His eye was upon his business in all its various branches; he mastered every detail and worked hard.

It has also been repeatedly asserted that Noah Webster never could have prepared his dictionary in thirty-six years, unless the most exacting method had come to the rescue. He himself claimed that his orderly methods saved him ten or twenty years, and a vast amount of anxiety and trouble.

Good habits are the first steps in order for children,—punctuality, neatness, a place for everything. Yet, do not let habits master you, so that you never can do anything except in a fixed manner at a fixed time, and cannot give up your way of doing for the sake of something greater.

It is true, however, that there is a wonderful force in mere regularity. A writer by the name of Bergh tells of a man beginning business, who opened and shut his store at the same hour every day for weeks, without selling two cents' worth of goods, yet whose application attracted attention and paved the way to fortune.

Sir Walter Scott has also said that "When a regiment is under march, the rear is often thrown into confusion because the front does not move steadily and without interruption. It is the same thing with business. If that which is first in hand be not instantly, steadily, and regularly dispatched, other things accumulate behind, till affairs begin to press all at once, and no human brain can stand the confusion."

The great enemy of order is laziness. It is too much trouble to do a thing when it ought to be done, instead of doing it when you want to do it. Young people should learn to think, talk, read in an orderly manner.

The country, the state, the town, the home, depend upon order. Supposing each person did what he wished, without regard to the welfare of others,— that meals, parties, lessons, came at any time; that caucuses and elections happened when any one desired them; that prisons and hospitals took people or not, just as superintendents felt; that everybody was a self-constituted policeman, yet no one wanted to be looked after himself;—what a hard time all people would have!

A very important point still remains to be noticed. It is this: Our principles ought to be strong enough to govern our habits. Habits may make us disagreeable and fussy; principles make us broad, far-seeing, sympathetic, and independent. Success in life depends upon having the *principle* of order. Always do the *important* thing *first*; for that is what order means. Some boys and girls are orderly about their rooms, but disorderly in their ways of doing things,—always in a hurry, and always puzzled what to do next. Orderly people make plans, allow a margin of time for carrying them out, so that they shall not overlap one duty with another; and then, if there is any time left, they fill it with some extra employment or enjoyment, which they have kept in the background all ready for use.

JOHN WESLEY.

If John Wesley had not been such an orderly boy, he never could have been the founder of Methodism. He was born at Epworth, England, in 1703, and had nineteen brothers and sisters, though only ten of them lived long enough to be educated.

His brother Charles was his intimate companion. When students at Oxford, they and two other friends formed a small society, which was called the "Holy Club" by those who laughed at it. They had sets of questions, labeled in order for their examination. From the exact regularity of their lives and their methods of study, they came to be called Methodists, in allusion to some ancient physicians who were so termed. The name was so quaint that it became immediately popular. They visited the poor and sick, and had regular lists of inquiries and rules for general use.

All the orderly habits of his youth guided him even when he became a man; and the amount of work he accomplished is almost beyond belief. In the last three years of his life, although sick nearly all the time, he preached as many times as ever until a week before his death, in 1791. Always anxious never to lose a moment, and to be methodical in all his habits, he read as he traveled on horseback for forty years. He delivered forty thousand sermons, and wrote many books and essays, and gave away in charity one hundred and fifty thousand dollars, which was a great sum in those days.

The secret of John Wesley's success began in his love of order, and culminated in the wonderful, orderly discipline of the immense Methodist denomination. At his death there were nearly eighty thousand members, whose leaders, great and little, had definite duties to perform. Yet, in his love for order, he never lost sight of individual poor and sick people, but remembered to serve each one.

[Footnote: See "Lives of Wesley," by Tyerman (1876); Riss (1875); Isaac Taylor's "Wesley and Methodism" (1868); and "Wesley's Journals," in seven volumes.]

XXVIII.

REVERENCE.

MEMORY GEMS.

Reverence is the crown of moral manhood.—C. Kingsley

No man of sound nature ever makes a mock of reverence.—T. T. Munger

True reverence is homage tempered by love.—W. B. Pope

In the full glow of the light of our times, only the pure are really revered.—Wilberforce

Reverence is alike indispensable to the happiness of individuals, of families, and of nations.—Smiles

Reverence is a word by itself. It has no synonyms, nor does any other word in the language exactly fill its place. It is not respect; it is not regard; it is not fear; it is not honor. Perhaps awe comes nearest to it; and yet reverence is more than awe. It is awe softened and refined by gentleness and love.

Reverence is a condition of thought and feeling which does not paralyze action, but kindles it; does not deaden sensibility, but quickens it. Even when used in a religious sense, reverence does not stand for religion itself, but as a means or aid to religious thought and life.

The presence or absence of a reverent spirit is of real importance; for it adds to, or takes away from, our enjoyment of the world in which we live. One person finds happiness everywhere and in every occasion; carrying his own holiday with him. Another always appears to be returning from a funeral. One sees beauty and harmony wherever he looks, while another is blind to beauty; the lenses of his eyes seem to be made of smoked glass, draping the whole world in mourning. While one man sees only gravel, fodder, and firewood, as he looks into a richly-wooded park; another is ravished with its beauty. One sees in a matchless rose nothing but an ordinary flower; another penetrates its purpose, and reads in the beauty of its blended colors and its wonderful fragrance the very thoughts of God.

Only the truly reverent soul can catch the higher music of sentient being, with its joys and hopes; its wealth of earnest, aspiring, struggling souls; tolerant, serious, yet sunny; and read those larger possibilities which lie hidden in the great deeps of the most ordinary human life.

While it is true that only the reverent can fully appreciate nature; it is even more true in regard to human nature. To the reverent mind an old man or woman is an object of tender regard; while by the irreverent, the aged are frequently treated with ingratitude, and sometimes even with contempt.

One of the lessons most frequently and most strongly impressed upon the Lacedaemonian youth, was to entertain great reverence and respect for old men, and to give them proof of it on all occasions, by saluting them; by making way for them, and giving them place in the streets; by rising up to show them honor in all companies and public assemblies; but, above all, by receiving their advice, and even their reproofs, with docility and submission.

On one occasion, when there was a great play at the principal theater in Athens, the seats set apart for strangers were filled with Spartan boys; and other seats, not far distant, were filled with Athenian youth. The theater was crowded, when an old man, infirm, and leaning on a staff, entered. There was no seat for him. The Athenian youth called to the old man to come to them, and with great difficulty he picked his way to their benches; but not a boy rose and offered him a seat. Seeing this, the Spartan boys beckoned to the old man to come to them, and, as he approached their benches, every Spartan boy rose, and, with uncovered head, stood until the old man was seated, and then all quietly resumed their seats. Seeing this, the Athenians broke out in loud applause. The old man rose, and, in a voice that filled the theater, said, "The Athenians know what is right: the Spartans do it."

The great German thinker, Goethe, claimed that three kinds of reverence should be taught to youth,—for superiors, for equals, and forinferiors. This was an advance over the old ideas; but, in a republic like ours, reverence is not up and down; it is not measured by class distinctions,—it is a spirit, to be related in sympathetic ways with all human beings as such; and especially with all whose lives are such as to command our respect and esteem.

Reverence can be cultivated, and needs to be cultivated in our times. There is too much mere "smartness" abroad. In society and in the world we find a flippant, cynical tone; no doubt much of this is reaction from old-time gloom and severity. But without a reasonable reverence we cannot have good manners, or loyal citizens, or possessors of really beautiful characters.

Reverence is developed by looking for the good in others; by avoiding fault-finding; by associating with high-minded acquaintances; by reading worthy literature; by using language unstained by vulgarity; by striving to enter more and more into the spirit of the noblest lives that come under our notice.

Reverence, then, is not fear; but wonder, solemnity, and veneration. "It is to cherish a habit of looking upward, and seeing what is noble and good in all things." Its blessings are many. By it we can win a masterly judgment to determine the fitness of behavior and habits; it will keep us from thoughtless words and deeds; it will make us respectful to old age and appreciative of the past; and, in many other ways, it will prove itself of real value to all who cultivate and cherish it.

HENRY WADSWORTH LONGFELLOW.

We select, as our special example, Henry Wadsworth Longfellow, the best known of our American poets. The great poet, whoever he may be, is always reverential. His stanzas are crowned with a sacred seriousness. He gives to life a "grand, true, harmonic interpretation." Longfellow was born on the 27th of February, 1807, at Portland, Maine. In his earlier years he displayed the same gentle, amiable spirit which filled his after-life with sunshine and goodness.

He proved himself to be possessed of a very bright mind even as a boy, and entered Bowdoin College when only fourteen years of age. He afterwards served this same institution as professor of modern languages, and in 1835 was called to fill a similar position in Harvard University.

He visited Europe, twice at least, for purposes of study; and, on his return from his second trip, began that illustrious career of instruction and authorship which has been the source of so much honorable pride on the part of his countrymen. Longfellow selected a historic home in Cambridge; it was the house occupied by Washington when he took command of the United States Army in 1776,—a spacious structure, full of welcoming windows, and situated in the midst of old elms. Here he lived till his death; and now the stretch of land, from the estate to the river Charles, has been bought and adorned as a memorial.

The writings of Longfellow are household possessions, fully as much in England as in America, and we need not enumerate them. They are famous not so much for originality, as for their calm, spiritual, purifying messages. They are full of good-will, aspiration, trust, and real loftiness of tone. Indeed, Longfellow "loved to make clear his discipleship to him whose ministry was love, whose flock was all humanity, whose kingdom was peace and righteousness."

So deep was the impression made by Mr. Longfellow's beauty of character, that it equaled his literary fame. He always responded to callers, and they came by hundreds; he never refused his autograph; children loved him; his charities were manifold; young authors received his encouragement. Modest as to his own writings, he strove to praise the good in others. Every one who met him perceived the source of all this rare grace and fascinating nobility of soul to be a sense of the glory and divineness of all life. His soul stood in a reverential attitude toward existence, and a marvelous light shone through him and his poetry as the result.

Down to the last his pen was active. He died on the 24th of March, 1882. Degrees and honors had been freely bestowed on him; but the highest tributes came from his admirers on both sides of the Atlantic; and his reverential spirit still lives in hundreds of those who read his beautiful verses.

[Footnote: See "Life of Longfellow," and "Final Memorials" both by his brother; Samuel Longfellow, and articles in all the best magazines.]

XXIX.

SENTIMENT.

MEMORY GEMS.

Sentiment is nothing but thought blended with feeling.—J. F. Clarke

Sentiment takes part in the shaping of all destinies.—R. Southey

A little child is the sweetest and purest thing in the world.
—J. S. White

Sentiment is the life and soul of poetry and art.—J. Flaxman

Sentiment is emotion precipitated in pretty crystals by the fancy.
—J. R. Lowell

It is quite difficult to define sentiment. This has been done, however, by the use of the following figures. "We may think of it as color, without which nothing in nature or art is complete. A colorless character is as unsatisfactory as a colorless landscape. We may also think of it as cement; for it serves to bind together the ordinary facts and incidents of life. Just as the bricks and stones of a building are useless until held in the places designed for them under some governing plan, so we may say that a selfish and gross character is not bound together by noble sentiments. Or we may say, again, that sentiment is the wing-power of man, whereby he has ability to fly away from the commonplace and unworthy. By it the ordinary citizen becomes a glowing patriot; the drudging youth turns into the devoted statesman; and life is made better in a thousand ways."

In one of our memory gems we find it asserted that "sentiment is the life and soul of poetry and art." Perhaps this statement may help us here. Pure poetry is the perfection of prose, or prose idealized. "It is a dream drawn from the infinite, and portrayed to mortal sense." It takes a great mind, a great genius to weave into a gossamer web, complete and perfect in every part, a story, a tale, an idea, which alike charms the mind, enthralls the sense, and enchains the spirit. Poetry is the perfection of language. It is not a mere mechanical contrivance of words, but a glorious picture in which the outward execution is lost in a glory of expression.

The poet Holmes was brimful of sentiment. Listen to him as he talks about the flowers.

"Do you ever wonder why poets talk so much about flowers? Did you ever hear of a poet who did not talk about them? Don't you think a poem, which, for the sake of being original, should leave them out, would be like those verses where the letter 'a' or 'e' or some other is omitted? No,—they will bloom over and over again in poems as in the summer fields, to the end of time, always old and always new.

"Are you tired of my trivial personalities,—those splashes and streaks of sentiment, sometimes perhaps of sentimentality, which you may see when I show you my heart's corolla as if it were a tulip? Pray, do not give yourself the trouble to fancy me an idiot, whose conceit it is to treat himself as an exceptional being. It is because you are just like me that I talk and know that you listen. We are all splashed and streaked with sentiments,—not with precisely the same tints, or in exactly the same patterns, but by the same hand and from the same palette."

To say, as some do, that there is no place for sentiment in life, would be almost equal to saying that life is devoid of joy. But who says there are no joys in life? Take, for example a good pure natural laugh. We hear it bubbling, gushing, pealing out, every now and then, from some glad child of nature; and we say, there *is* joy in life. The gloom of ages has been lightened with laughter and song.

There is much to awaken deep and real sentiment in us as we gaze on the tree-tops, the mountains and hillsides, the gurgling waters and sweeping billows; on sunlight, shadow, and storm. Behind the forest-leaf we suddenly discover a songster, the gleam of an oriole's breast in a bed of mantling green. Nature always rejoices. She has been singing and laughing all down the ages. She does her part grandly for the happiness of man; and as we come into closer touch with her, sentiment arises as naturally in our hearts, as does the water in her bubbling springs.

We may find a place for sentiment in all life's changeful affairs. Even the stern realities of war do not entirely eradicate from the heart that feeling for suffering humanity, which is the highest expression of sentiment.

There were but few who were so thoughtless as not to be stirred with the feeling which possessed the heart of Captain Phillips, and the crew of the battleship Texas, when, as they stood on the deck, with uncovered heads and reverent souls, on the afternoon of the engagement before Santiago, the knightly old sailor said: "I want to make public acknowledgment here that I believe in God. I want all you officers and men to lift your hats, and from your hearts offer silent thanks to the Almighty for the victory he has given us." But it was not the mere victory over a foe that caused this general and thoughtful lifting of heart; it was exultation at the triumph of justice and the progress of freedom.

The presence or absence of sentiment in our lives is largely accounted for by the fact that we usually find what we are looking for. The geologist sees design and order in the very stones with which the streets are paved. The botanist reads volumes in the flowers and grasses which most men tread thoughtlessly beneath their feet. The astronomer gazes with rapt soul into the starry heavens, while his fellows seldom glance upward. If we seek for the beautiful and the pure, it will be quickly revealed to us; and the sentiment of loving gratitude will arise within us as the result.

Nature takes on our moods; she laughs with those who laugh, and weeps with those who weep. If we rejoice and are glad, the very birds sing more sweetly; the woods and streams murmur our song. But if we are sad and sorrowful, a sudden gloom falls upon nature's face; the sun shines, but not in our hearts; the birds sing, but not to us. The beauty of nature's music is lost to us, and everything seems dull and gray. The lack of sentiment narrows and belittles us; and, for that reason, we cannot afford to be without it.

We must always strive to keep in mind how important sentiment is to a happy and useful career, whatever position in life we may happen to occupy. Noble sentiments are the richest possession we can have. They cheer us when we are despondent, they sing to us when we are lonesome, and they help to keep us young. They are like brilliant poets and divine musicians; by whom the true, the good, and the beautiful are kept constantly before our minds.

It is this trait of character which has to do greatly with worship, reverence, and aspiration. Morality needs to be touched by sentiment or emotion. Sentiment leads us to love sacred spots, to create commemorative days, and to sing songs of gratitude together. It makes life of far greater worth to us in every way. We must also glance at what is known as public sentiment. Public sentiment is not voluntary or self-creative. It is generally a thing of slow growth, springing from a gradual accumulation and development of evidences, impressions, and circumstances. It is a matter of education, impressed upon the masses by the most intelligent or the most influential forces of a community; and as it is often merely the adoption by the masses of the opinions of a class, clique, or ring, it is as likely to be wrong as right, since it frequently serves to popularize evils, the existence and the continuance of which, minister only to the benefit of a few.

But public sentiment, is after all, quite largely a personal matter. We all help in making it; and we should therefore be exceedingly careful as to the sentiments we personally cherish; for these are a very real part of the sentiments of the community as a whole.

BEETHOVEN.

Perhaps we should be safe in saying that the kingdom of music is especially the realm of sentiment. Music raises us to a loftier plane of thought and feeling. It has been beautifully said that "The composer's world is the world of emotion; full of delicate elations and depressions, which like the hum of minute insects hardly arrest the uncultivated ear."

We select as our special illustration Ludwig van Beethoven, who was born at Bonn, Prussia, in the year 1770. His father was a musician, and suffered from two great foes,—a violent temper, and a habit of drink. The family being poor, young Ludwig was made to submit to a severe training on the violin from the time he was four years old, in order to obtain money. By the time he reached the age of nine, he had advanced so far in music that his father could not teach him anything more, and he was passed over to others for further education. When he was fifteen years old he was appointed assistant to the court organist; and, in a description of the various musicians attached to the court, he is described as "of good capacity, young, of good, quiet behavior, and poor."

At the court he was an object of admiration, and his popularity was constantly on the increase. Absorbed in meditation, he forgot ordinary affairs. One illustration is as good as a dozen. He loved the sound of flowing water, and frequently would let it run over his hands until, lost in some musical suggestion from the murmur, he would allow the water to pour over the floor of his apartment until it soaked down and astonished the dwellers below.

He was very democratic, and desired that all men should enjoy freedom and equal rights before the law. When asked once, in court, to produce the proof of his nobility, he pointed to his head and heart, saying, "My nobility is here, and here." His high-strung nervous system would account for many of his peculiarities. By those who did not understand him he was called "a growling old bear." On the other hand, those who appreciated his genius called him "a cloud-compeller of the world of music." He is in music what Milton is in poetry,—lofty, majestic, stately.

Beethoven died on March 26, 1827, during a terrible thunderstorm. His funeral was attended by all the musicians of Vienna. The crowd of people was so enormous that soldiers had to be called in to make a way for the procession; and it took an hour and a half to pass the little distance from the house to the church.

Sentiment in music leaves one in an uplifted and wholesome state of mind. Sentimentality in music may give a momentary pleasure, but it is really hostile to strength of character; and this truth applies, with equal force, to every other feature of our lives.

[Footnote: See Thayer's "Biography of Beethoven" (1879); Schindler's "Beethoven;" and Grove's "Dictionary of Music and Musicians." Magazine articles on Beethoven are also numerous.]

XXX.

DUTY.

MEMORY GEMS.

The path of duty is the way to glory.—Tennyson

A sense of duty pursues us ever and everywhere.—Webster

The consciousness of duty performed "gives us music at midnight."
—George Herbert

I slept and dreamed that life was Beauty.
I woke and found that life was Duty.—E. S. Hooper

Let us have faith that right makes might; and in that faith let us dare
to do our duty as we understand it.—A. Lincoln

Samuel Smiles, who has written a most excellent book upon this subject, says, "Duty is the end and aim of the highest life; and it alone is true." It is certain that of all the watchwords of life, duty is the highest and best. He who sincerely adopts it lives a true life; he is really the successful man. It pertains to all parts and relations of life. There is no moment, place, or condition where its claims are not imperative.

Obedience to the commands of duty, and the ruling desire to be useful, are cardinal elements of success. It is at the trumpet call which duty sounds, that all the nobler attributes of manhood spring into life; and duty is something that must be done without regard to discomfort, sacrifice, or death. It must be done in secret, as well as in public; and according to the measure of our faithfulness in this respect, will be the real measure of our manhood.

History and biography are fairly crowded with examples of the faithful performance of duty, and the glorious results which have followed; such as Nelson at Trafalgar, Luther at the Diet of Worms, General Grant in the Civil War; and scores of other instances of note. But equally valuable are the cases of ordinary life. The engineer on the locomotive; the pilot at the helm of the storm-tossed vessel; the mother in her daily routine of work; the merchant upholding laws of trade in honor; the schoolboy plodding through studies in a manly thoroughness; the reformer of slums letting her little candle of service shine in the dark;—all these and similar instances are full of guidance and inspiration.

There are two aspects of duty; namely, cheerful duty and drudging duty. One says, "I want to do something;" the other says, "I must." Our New England forefathers were followers of duty, but they found very little joy in it, as we understand that word. We should endeavor to improve upon their methods, but we shall find it difficult to improve upon their faithfulness.

The life of Sir Walter Scott affords an interesting illustration of strict obedience to the line of duty. His whole life seems to have been governed by that sense of obligation which caused him, when a young man, to enter a profession which he heartily disliked, out of affection for his father; and, later in life, to set himself to paying off the debt incurred by the publishing house of which he was a silent partner. His sense of duty was expressed in his declaration that, "If he lived and retained his health, no man should lose a penny by him."

Just what is meant by faithfulness to duty may be clearly seen in the following incident. During the famous *dark day* of 1780, in Connecticut, candles were lighted in many houses, and domestic fowls went to their roosts. The people thought the day of judgment had come. The legislature was then in session in Hartford. The house of representatives adjourned. In the council, which corresponds to the modern senate, an adjournment was also proposed. Colonel Davenport objected, saying, "The day of judgment is either approaching, or it is not. If it is not, there is no cause for adjourning; if it is, I choose to be found doing my duty. I wish, therefore, that candles may be brought."

Upon the world's great battlefields, this matter of faithfulness to duty has always been deemed of the first importance. Previous to the battle of Lutzen, in which eighty thousand Austrians were defeated by an army of thirty-six thousand Prussians, commanded by Frederick the Great, this monarch ordered all his officers to attend him, and thus addressed them: "To-morrow I intend giving the enemy battle; and, as it will decide who are to be the future masters of Silesia, I expect every one of you, in the strictest manner, to do his duty. If any one of you is a coward, let him step forward before he makes others as cowardly as himself,—let him step forward, I say, and he shall immediately receive his discharge without ceremony or reproach. I see there is none among you who does not possess true heroism, and will not display it in defense of his king, of his country, and of himself. I shall be in the front and in the rear; shall fly from wing to wing; no company will escape my notice; and whoever I then find doing his duty, upon him will I heap honor and favor."

Another great military commander was the Duke of Wellington. He once said to a friend: "There is little or nothing in this life worth living for; but we can all of us go straight forward and do our duty." Whether serving at home in his family, or serving his country on the field, his sense of duty was the one high and noble purpose that inspired him. He did not ask, Will this course win fame? Will this battle add to my earthly glory? But always, What is my duty? He did what duty commanded, and followed where it led. It was his firm adherence to what he thought was right, that brought down upon him the violence of a mob in the streets of London, assaulting his person and attacking his house, even while his wife lay dead therein. But the memory of few men is now more greatly honored; and his example is worthy of careful study and close imitation.

The foregoing facts show, far better than argument, both the nature and place of duty in the work of life. We see it in practical operation, always timely, honorable, and attractive. It cannot be discounted or even smirched. It stands out in bold relief, supported by a clear conscience and strong will. It demands recognition, and it always secures it.

More than sixteen hundred years after an eruption of Vesuvius had buried Pompeii in ashes, explorers laid bare the ruins of the ill-fated city. There the unfortunate inhabitants were found just where they were overtaken by death. Some were discovered in lofty attics and some in deep cellars, whither they had fled before the approaching desolation. Others were found in the streets, through which they were fleeing in wild despair when the tide of volcanic gases and the storm of falling ashes overwhelmed them. But the Roman sentinel was standing at his post, his skeleton-hand still grasping the hilt of his sword, his attitude that of a faithful officer. He was placed there on duty, and death met him at his post.

No man has a right to say he can do nothing for the benefit of mankind. We forget that men are less benefited by ambitious projects, than by the sober fulfillment of each man's proper duties. By doing the proper duty, in the proper time and place, a man may make the entire world his debtor, and may accomplish far more of good than in any other way.

LORD NELSON.

Horatio Nelson was born at Norfolk, England, September 29, 1758. He reached his manhood at a time when the nations of Europe were engaged in deadly strife. A love of adventure and a daring spirit, which developed during his earliest years, inclined him to follow the sea. From his first entrance into this calling, genius and opportunity worked together to make him the leading factor in Great Britain's prominence as a naval power.

For several centuries, previous to the time of Nelson, Great Britain had been rapidly advancing her commerce. In the protection of this commerce many a naval hero won renown; but the tide of influence and of power found in Nelson its perfect fulfillment. He was a man of extraordinary genius. He saw clearly; acted vigorously. He felt that it was his business and his duty to watch over England's interests upon the sea; and both men and women felt perfectly safe while Nelson had command. The pure flame of patriotism burned brightly in his heroic soul. He believed, with Lord Sandon, that nothing could be nobler than a first-rate English sailor; and he acted in strict accord with this belief. He attained one victory after another, until the battle of the Nile, one of his most brilliant successes, made the navy of England a terror even to its bravest enemies. The superiority of the English fleet was mainly due to his genius; and the dread his name inspired was one of the principal causes, that, a few years later, kept Napoleon from carrying out his threatened invasion of England.

His high sense of duty, and what he expected of those under his command, is well illustrated by his signal to the English fleet, when they were about to engage the French in the great naval battle at Trafalgar. When all were ready for the attack, Nelson said, "I will now amuse the fleet with a signal." Turning to the signal officer he exclaimed, "Send this message,—'England expects every man to do his duty.'" When the signal was comprehended by the men, cheer after cheer rang out upon the air, and under its inspiration they won a glorious and a decisive victory.

This message was characteristic of Nelson. Upon his entering into this engagement, which proved to be his last, he is said to have remarked, "I thank God for this great opportunity of doing my duty." While in the thick of the engagement, Nelson was struck down by a cannon ball, and lived but a few hours afterward; but long enough to hear the English shouts of triumph. He had left to the world a type of single-minded self-devotion, that can never perish.

[Footnote: See "Life of Nelson," by Southey (1828); "Letters and Dispatches of Lord Nelson," by N. H. Nicols (1860); "Lady Hamilton and Lord Nelson," by J. C. Jeaffreson; and Mahan's "Life of Nelson," recently published.]

XXXI.

TEMPERANCE.

MEMORY GEMS.

Rum will brutalize the manliest man in Christendom.-J. B. Gough

Rum excites all that is bad, vicious, and criminal in man.-J. S. White

There may be some wit in a barrel of beer, but there is more in leaving it alone.-C. Garrett

Sobriety is the bridle of the passions of desire, and temperance is the bit and curb of that bridle; a restraint put into a man's mouth; a moderate use of meat and drink.-Jeremy Taylor

Temperance is corporeal piety; it is the preservation of divine order in the body.-Theodore Parker

Temperance may, in its narrower sense, be defined as the observance of a rational medium with respect to the pleasures of eating and drinking. But it has also a larger meaning. The temperate man desires to hold all his pleasures within the limits of what is honorable, and with a proper reference to the amount of his own pecuniary means. To pursue them more is excess; to pursue them less is defect. There is, however, in estimating excess and defect, a certain tacit reference to the average dispositions of men, and the law of usage or custom of the times.

The word temperance has, we repeat, become narrowed and specialized. We mean by it, not exactly temperance, but abstinence. The word does not convey the full force of its older meaning. That signifies, "the right handling of one's self,—that kind of self-control by which a man's nature has a chance to act normally;" and this aspect of our subject must not be overlooked, for it is of great importance.

Instead of being the secondary thing which some think it to be, temperance is really a much higher virtue than patience or fortitude. It is the guardian of reason, the bulwark of religion, the sister of prudence, and the sweetener of life. Be temperate; and time will carry you forward on its purest current till it lands you on the continent of a yet purer eternity, as the swelling river rolls its limpid stream into the bosom of the unfathomable deep.

But even in the more general meaning now given to the word, temperance is worthy of our most careful study.

Consider what it is to gain the mastery over a single passion! And think, also, what it is for the mind to be ruled by an appetite! Look at S. T. Coleridge—a poet who might have sung for all time, a philosopher capable of teaching and molding generations, skulking away from the eye of friends and of servants to drink his bottle of laudanum, and then bewailing his weakness and sin with an agony, the bare recital of which, makes our hearts bleed with pity. Our task is not only to subdue a serpent, to tame a lion,—there is a whole menagerie of evil passions to be kept in subjection, and when the drink habit prevails, we shall soon become too weak for such a task.

Temperance is an action; it is the tempering of our words and actions to our circumstances. Sobriety is a state in which one is exempt from every stimulus to deviate from the right course. As a man who is intoxicated with wine, runs into excesses, and loses that power of guiding himself which he has when he is sober or free from all intoxication, so is he who is intoxicated with any passion, led into irregularities which a man in his right senses will not be guilty of. Sobriety is, therefore, the state of being in one's right or sober senses; and sobriety is, with regard to temperance, as a cause to its effect.

The evils resulting from intemperance are so numerous and so destructive of human happiness and life, as to command universal attention. Not only does intemperance greatly increase pauperism and crime, but it often leads to sad calamities which might otherwise be quite largely avoided.

An old English sea-captain relates the following fact, of which he was an eyewitness:—"A collier brig was stranded on the Yorkshire coast, and I had occasion to assist in the distressing service of rescuing a part of the crew by drawing them up a vertical cliff, two or three hundred feet in altitude, by means of a very small rope, the only material at hand. The first two men who caught hold of the rope were hauled safely up to the top; but the next, after being drawn to a considerable height, slipped his hold and fell; and with the fourth and last who venturedupon this only chance of life, the rope gave way, and he also was plunged into the foaming breakers beneath. Immediately afterward, the vessel broke up, and the remainder of the ill-fated crew perished before our eyes.

"What now was the cause of this heart-rending event? Was it stress of weather, or a contrary wind, or unavoidable accident? No such thing! It was the entire want of moral conduct in the crew. Every sailor, to a man, was in a state of intoxication! The helm was intrusted to a boy ignorant of the coast. He ran the vessel upon the rocks at Whitby; and one half of the miserable, dissipated crew were plunged into eternity almost without a knowledge of what was taking place."

There are still a few people who openly ridicule both total abstinence and its advocates, and some, who are wicked enough to endeavor to misrepresent those who labor in this cause. These persons do not always succeed, however, as the following incident will show: Horace Greeley was once met at a railway depot by a red-faced individual, who shook him warmly by the hand. "I don't recognize you," said Mr. Greeley. "Why, yes, you must remember how we drank brandy and water together at a certain place." This amused the bystanders, who knew Mr. Greeley's strong temperance principles. "Oh, I see," replied Mr. Greeley, "you drank the brandy, and I drank the water."

It will be found that abstinence from intoxicants is by far the best rule of living. There is a large amount of genuine wisdom in the words of a middle-aged German who, some years ago, spoke as follows, at a temperance meeting: "I shall tell you how it vas. I put my hand on my head; there was von big pain. Then I put my hand on my pody; and there vas another big pain. There was very much pains in all my pody. Then I put my hand in my pocket; and there vas noting. Now there is no more pain in my head. The pains in my pody are all gone away. I put mine hand in my pocket, and there ish twenty tollars. So I shall shtay mit de temperance."

FATHER MATHEW.

Theobald Mathew was an Irish priest. He was born in 1790, in a great house in Tipperary, where his father was the agent of a rich lord. The delight of his childhood was in giving little feasts and entertainments to his friends. As long as he lived he was fond of this pleasure. Indeed, when, at the very last, his physician had forbidden him to receive company, he was found by his brother giving a dinner to a party of poor boys.

At twenty-three years of age he was ordained, and was known from that time as "Father Mathew." After a short time in Kilkenny, he went to Cork, which was his home for the rest of his life. He was not thought much of as a scholar, nor at first as a preacher; but he had a warm heart and every one liked him. Thus he passed quietly along until he was forty-seven years old; and it did not seem as if the world would ever hear of "Father Mathew."

There was a little band of Quakers in Cork, who had started a total abstinence, or "teetotal society." They interested Father Mathew in their work, and, in 1838, he signed the temperance pledge and enrolled himself as a member.

Very soon every one in Cork had heard of what Father Mathew had done. He began at once to preach that men ought not to be drunkards, and that they ought not to use what would make drunkards. The people of Cork had always thought what Father Mathew did was right; and they thought so now. In three months twenty-five thousand persons had taken the pledge.

The story of the new movement spread quickly over Ireland, and Father Mathew was wanted everywhere. Wherever he went the people crowded to hear him. There were many pathetic scenes at his meetings; for women came dragging their drunken husbands with them, and almost forcing them to take the pledge. Men knelt in great companies and repeated the words of the pledge together. In Limerick the crowds were so dense that it was impossible to enroll all the names. More than a hundred thousand were thought to have taken the pledge in four days.

As a result of his work the saloons were closed in many villages and towns; and, within five years, half the people in Ireland had taken the pledge. The quantity of liquor used fell off more than half, and there was a similar decrease in all kinds of crime.

Then came the terrible years of the Irish famine. By the failure of the potato crop, hundreds of thousands died of starvation or of fever. Multitudes had to leave their homes to get government work; and hunger and despair brought a new temptation to drink. Father Mathew's heart was well-nigh broken with seeing the misery of his countrymen. The food was taken from his own table to feed the hungry. Every room in his house would sometimes be filled with poor people clamoring for bread; and, largely as a result of this terrible strain, he was stricken with paralysis.

As soon as Father Mathew had partly recovered from his illness he longed to do something for his people across the sea. In the year 1849 he sailed for New York. The mayor of that city made him an address of welcome; and at Washington he was honored by being admitted to the floor of both houses of Congress. In spite of his broken health, he visited twenty-five states, spoke in over three hundred towns and cities, and gave the pledge to five hundred thousand people. He returned home thoroughly exhausted, and soon had another stroke of paralysis. But loving friends cared for him; people still came for his blessing, or to take the pledge in his presence. He died in 1856, and all the people of Cork followed him to his burial.

It is said that seven million people took the pledge of total abstinence at Father Mathew's hands; and it is thought that hundreds of thousands never broke it. There is now a new feeling about temperance in the English-speaking world. Drunkenness is now looked upon as a disgrace; total abstinence is becoming the habit of increasing numbers of people from year to year; and in the production of this changed feeling, this simple-hearted, earnest Irish priest did more than any other man.

[Footnote: See "Father Mathew, his Life and Times," by F. J. Mathew (Cassell & Co., 1880), and "Biography of Father Mathew," by J. F. Maguire, M. P. (London, 1863).]

XXXII.

PATRIOTISM.

MEMORY GEMS.

The noblest motive is the public good.—Virgil

The one best omen is to fight for fatherland.—Homer

Patriotism is a principle fraught with high impulses and noble thoughts.—Smiles

The revolutionist has seldom any other object but to sacrifice his country to himself.—Alison

It is impossible that a man who is false to his friends should be true to his country.—Bishop Berkeley

Patriotism is defined by Noah Webster as "the passion which aims to serve one's country." As it is natural to love our home, it is natural to love our country also. As the poorest homes are sometimes most tenderly loved, so the poorest and barest country is sometimes held in most affection. There is, perhaps, not a country in the world the inhabitants of which have not, at some time or other, been willing to suffer and die for it.

But as we think of our land, we quickly perceive that no body of young people ever had a more valuable inheritance than that which we have received; and we are under the greatest obligations to protect and preserve this land, and transmit it, full of the grandest achievements and most glorious recollections, to posterity.

This affection is natural, because the town and the nation in which one has lived, is, like the home, bound up with all the experiences of one's life. The games of childhood, the affection of parents, the love of friends, all the joys, the sorrows, the activities of life, are bound up in the thought of one's native land.

It is not merely natural to be patriotic, but it is also reasonable and right. Nearly all that makes life pleasant and desirable, comes to us through the town or the nation to which we belong. Think how many thousands in our country have toiled for us! They have made roads, and they have built churches and schoolhouses. They have established malls and post offices. They have cultivated farms to provide for our needs, and have built ships that cross the ocean to bring to us the good things which we could not produce at home. They have provided protection against wrongdoers; so that if we sleep in peace, and work and study and play in safety, we are indebted for all this to the town and nation.

When the bells are ringing, and the cannons are firing, on the Fourth of July, we must not think merely of the noise and fun. We must remember those who on that day agreed that they would risk their lives and everything that was dear to them, that their country might be free. We must also think of those who in times of peril have given themselves for their nation's good; of those who found the land a wilderness, and suffered pain and privation while they made the beginning of a nation. We must think of those who, ever since that time, when ever the liberty or the unity of the nation has been in peril, have sprung to its defense.

At the end of the war of the revolution, Washington was at the head of a mighty army, and was the object of the enthusiastic love of the whole people. He might easily have made himself a king or an emperor. It was a marvel to the civilized world when he quietly laid down all his power. He suffered himself to be twice chosen president; and then he became simply a private citizen. This seems to us now the most natural thing in the world; but really it was something very rare, and gave him a fame such as few heroes of the world enjoy.

There have been heroes in peace as well as in war, men who have conquered the wilderness, who have upheld justice, and have helped on whatever was good and noble. And there are also many persons among us who are unworthy to live in our country, because they are not willing to suffer the least inconvenience on its account.

Then there are many men who are even so unpatriotic as to sell their votes. Think of all the cost of money and of noble lives at which our liberty has been won. Think how, in many parts of the world, men are looking with longing at the liberty which we enjoy; yet there are those to whom this hard-won freedom means so little that they do not strive to further the country's interests in any way.

We must never forget, as we think or speak of patriotism, that such private virtues as honesty and industry, are its best helps. Whatever tends to make men wiser and better is a service to the nation. The country will one day be in the hands of those who are now boys and girls; and to you, we say, serve it, guard it, and do all that you can to promote its good.

There is a fine field for the exercise of patriotism in trying to improve the condition of affairs in the towns and cities in which we live. We find ourselves in the midst of a conflict between the criminal classes on the one hand, and the people on the other,—a conflict as stern as was ever endured upon the battlefield, amid the glitter of cold steel and the rattle of musketry.

The man or woman of the school committee, working conscientiously that the boys and girls shall have the best education to fit them for future life, is a patriot. The teacher who patiently works on with that great end in view, is the same. If greed or bigotry claims from town, city, or country, that which will debase her people, every boy and girl, every man and woman, should instantly frown it down. This is true patriotism, and the influence of every person is needed for the right.

Every good man in politics wields a power for good. Every good man not in politics is to blame for political corruption, because by neglecting his plain duty he adds to the strength of the enemy. Let it be known that, with you, principle amounts to something; that character counts; that questionable party service cannot count upon your suffrage.

JOHN ADAMS.

But little has been written of the child-life of John Adams, the second president of the United States; a man of unflinching honesty, and a patriot of the noblest order.

The Adamses were an honest, faithful people. They were not rich, neither were they poor; but being thrifty and economical, they lived with comfort. Stern integrity was the predominant quality of the farmer's home into which John Adams was born in 1735. It must be remembered, throughout his life it was the sturdy qualities of his ancestors that made him the statesman and patriot whom we know.

The boy did not show much fondness for books. He preferred life out of doors among the birds and the squirrels, roaming the woods,—living just the life a wide-awake boy on a farm would lead nowadays.

His father gave him the opportunity of a liberal education, and he entered Harvard College when he was sixteen years old. It is curious to note that the students were all enrolled according to social position, and John Adams was the fourteenth in his class. In college he was noted for integrity and energy as well as for ability,—those qualities which the sturdy line of farmers had handed down to their children.

The year he graduated, then twenty years of age, he became teacher of the grammar school in Worcester, Massachusetts. There he earned the money to aid him in studying his profession, and the training was excellent for the young man. He decided that he would be a lawyer, and he wrote: "But I set out with firm resolutions, never to commit any meanness or injustice in the practice of law."

There were stirring times in the colonies when John Adams was thirty years old. The British government imposed taxes and searched for goods which had evaded their officers. The matter was brought before the Superior Court. James Otis argued the cause of the merchants; and John Adams listened intently to all this great man said. He afterwards wrote: "Otis was a flame of fire.... American independence was then and there born. Every man appeared to be ready to get away and to take up arms."

Then the Stamp Act was issued. John Adams's whole soul was fired with indignation at the injustice. He drew up a set of resolutions, remonstrating against it. These were adopted, not only by the citizens of Braintree, but by those of more than forty other towns in Massachusetts; and the landing of the Stamp Act paper was prevented. Courts were closed, and the excitement was intense. John Adams boldly said that the Stamp Act was an assumption of arbitrary power, violating both the English constitution and the charter of the province.

In connection with what is known as "The Boston Tea Party," came the closing of Boston's ports, because the tea had been thrown overboard, and the city would not submit to the tax. A Congress was convened in Philadelphia, and John Adams was one of the five delegates sent from Boston. He knew the grave responsibility of the time. With intense feeling he exclaimed: "God grant us wisdom and fortitude! Should this country submit, what infamy and ruin! Death in any form is less terrible!"

Jefferson and Adams were appointed to draw up the Declaration of Independence. Mr. Adams insisted that Jefferson should prepare it, and he with forty-four others signed it. Mr. Jefferson wrote: "The great pillar of support to the Declaration of Independence, and its ablest advocate and champion on the floor of the House, was John Adams. He was our Colossus."

In various ways, John Adams served his country with unswerving loyalty. When Washington was chosen president, Adams was chosen vice-president for both terms, and was then elected president. To the very last he was always ready to give his word—strong, convincing, powerful as of old—in the defense of the right, even if he had to stand entirely alone. And the story of his manly independence will always add to the dignity of the early history of our nation.

[Footnote: See "Life and Works of John Adams," by C. F. Adams (10 vols.); "Life of John Adams," by J. T. Morse; and article in Appleton's Cyclopedia of American Biography, Vol. I., pp. 15-23.]

XXXIII.

INDEPENDENCE.

MEMORY GEMS.

Keep out of the crowd, if you have to get above it.—M. C Peters

The freedom of the mind is the highest form of independence.—G. B. Fisk

A country cannot subsist without liberty, nor liberty without virtue.
—Rousseau

The spirit of independence is not merely a jealousy of our own
particular rights, but a respect for the rights of others.
—S. Baring-Gould

The love of independence is not only instinctive in man, but its
possession is essential to his moral development.—George Eliot

A great many persons carry in their minds a very mistaken idea as to what constitutes a truly noble life. To live is not merely to exist; it is to live unbiased and uninfluenced by low and belittling human influences. It is to give breadth and expansion to the soul; first through a clear discrimination between right and wrong; and then in living up to the right. Full manhood, the full realization and fruition of all that is best and greatest in man, depends upon freedom of thought and independence of action.

Some countries have given especial attention to the cultivation of this trait. For example: It has been pointed out that "among the bestproducts of Scotland has been her love of independence. A ruggedness of spirit has marked her children. Strength stamps her heroes. The gentle Burns was as strong as Knox,—not in character, but in the assertion of 'A man's a man for a' that;' and a great many of Scotland's noblest sons have been brought into public notice through the manifestation of their strong personality."

Vast numbers of men and women ruin their lives by failing to assert themselves. They sink into the grave with scarcely a trace to indicate that they ever lived. They live and they die. Cradle and grave are brought close together; there is nothing between them. There have been hundreds who could have rivaled the patriotism of a Washington, or the humanity of a Howard, or the eloquence of a Demosthenes, and who have left behind them no one memorial of their existence, because of lack of lofty courage, sublime moral heroism, and the assertion of their individuality.

The world's greatest things have been accomplished by individuals. Vast social reformations have originated in individual souls. Truths that now sway the world were first proclaimed by individual lips. Great thoughts that are now the axioms of humanity sprang from the center of individual hearts. Do not suffer others to shape your lives for you; but do all you can to shape them for yourselves.

Sydney Smith insisted upon this quality of manhood and womanhood as indispensable. He said: "There is one circumstance I would preach up morning, noon, and night, to young persons for the management of their understanding: Whatever you are by nature, keep to it; never desert your own line of talent. Be what Nature intended you for, and you will succeed; be anything else, and you will be ten thousand times worse than nothing."

It is a good thing for a boy to wait upon himself as much as possible. The more he has to depend upon his own exertions, the more manly a fellow will he become. Self-dependence will call out his energies, and bring into exercise his talents. It is not in the hothouse, but on the rugged Alpine cliffs, where the storms beat most violently, that the toughest plants grow. So it is with man. The wisest charity is to help a boy to help himself. Let him never hear any language but this: You have your own way to make, and it depends on your own exertion whether you succeed or fail.

Sherman once wrote to General Grant, "You are now Washington's legitimate successor, and occupy a position of almost dangerous elevation; but if you continue, as heretofore, *to be yourself,*— simple, honest, and unpretending,—you will enjoy through life the respect and love of friends, and the homage of millions of human beings."

Of course we must guard against the error of carrying our sense of independence too far. Wordsworth hit the truth when he said: "These two things, contradictory as they may seem, must go together,—manly dependence and manly independence,—manly reliance and manly self-reliance."

Still, after all is said, we do need more healthy independence. Looking out upon society, we see how slavish men and women are to fashion and frivolity. Society life is largely a surface life, spoiled by fear of gossip. Young people need to take clearer views of this matter, and to stand by their own convictions at any cost. The question to be settled by most of us is, Shall I steer or drift? Our advice is, by all means have a lofty purpose before you, and then remain loyal to it.

Some boys think independence consists in doing whatever they please. They think it is smart to be "tough." A story told by Admiral Farragut about his early boyhood, aptly illustrates this phase of young America's independence. He says: "When I was a boy, ten years of age, I was with my father on board of a man-of-war. I had some qualities that I thought made a man of me. I could swear like an old salt; could drink as stiff a glass of grog as if I had doubled Cape Horn; and could smoke like a locomotive. I was great at cards; and fond of gaming in any shape. At the close of dinner one day my father turned everybody out of the cabin, locked the door, and said to me: 'David, what do you mean to be?' 'I mean to follow the sea.' 'Follow the sea! yes, to be a poor, miserable, drunken sailor before the mast; be kicked and cuffed about the world; and die in some fever hospital in a foreign clime.' 'No,' said I, 'I'll tread the quarter-deck, and command as you do.' 'No, David; no boy ever trod the quarter-deck with such principles as you have. You'll have to change your whole course of life if you ever become a man.'

"My father left me and went on deck. I was stunned by the rebuke, and overwhelmed with mortification. 'A poor, miserable, drunken sailor before the mast!' That's my fate, is it! I'll change my life, and change it at once! I will never utter another oath; I will never drink another drop of intoxicating liquor; I will never gamble! I have kept these three vows to this very hour. That was the turning point in my destiny."

A great many men begin to lose their individuality of conviction the moment they begin life's business. Many a young man has sacrificed his individuality on the altar that a profligate companion has built for him. Many a young man who knew right, has allowed some empty-headed street-corner loafer to lower his own high moral tone lest he should seem singular in the little world of society surrounding him. And many a lad whose life promised well at the beginning, has gone to the bad, or lost his chance in life, because he never learned to say "No!"

In the Revolutionary War, after the surrender of General Lincoln, at Charleston, the whole of South Carolina was overrun by the British army. Among those captured by the redcoats was a small boy, thirteen years of age. He was carried as a prisoner of war to Camden. While there, a British officer, in a very imperious tone, ordered the boy to clean his boots, which were covered with mud.

"Here, boy! You young rebel, what are you doing there? Take these boots and clean them; and be quick about it, too!"

The boy looked up at him and said: "Sir, I won't do it. I am a prisoner of war, and expect proper treatment from you, sir." This boy was Andrew Jackson, who afterward became president of the United States. Boys with such a spirit make noble men.

Exaggerated individuality makes a man impracticable. But the danger of our times is to copy after others, and thus destroy our force and effectiveness. Live, then, like an individual. Take life like a man—as though the world had waited for your coming. Don't take your cue from the weak, the prejudiced, the trimmers, the cowards;—but rather from the illustrious ones of earth.

Dare to take the side that seems wrong to others, if it seems right to you; and you will attain to an order of life the most noble and complete.

THOMAS JEFFERSON.

For the last one hundred years, one of the first historical facts taught the youth of American birth, is that Thomas Jefferson wrote our famous Declaration of Independence. His bold, free, independent nature, admirably fitted him for the writing of this remarkable document. To him was given the task of embodying, in written language, the sentiments and the principles for which, at that moment, a liberty-loving people were battling with their lives. He succeeded, because he wrote the Declaration while his heart burned with that same patriotic fire which Patrick Henry so eloquently expressed when he said: "I care not what others may do, but as for me, give me liberty or give me death."

In all nations men have sacrificed everything they held dear for religious and political freedom. Their names are justly written in the book of fame; but in the front rank of them all, we place the brave signers of the Declaration of Independence, with Jefferson in the lead.

The acceptance and the signing of this document by the members of the Continental Congress was a dramatic scene, seldom, if ever, surpassed in the annals of history. As John Hancock placed his great familiar signature upon it, he jestingly remarked, that John Bull could read that without spectacles; and then, becoming more serious, he began to impress upon his comrades the necessity of all hanging together in this matter. "Yes, indeed," interrupted Franklin, "we must all hang together, or assuredly we shall all hang separately."

The Declaration of Independence placed the American colonies squarely upon the issue of political freedom. Its composition was a master-stroke which will continue as a lasting memorial to the head and heart of its author.

[Footnote: See "Thomas Jefferson," by J. T. Morse, Jr. (in American Statesmen Series), and "Domestic Life of Thomas Jefferson," by Sarah N. Randolph, his great-granddaughter.]

XXXIV.

THE IDEAL MAN.

MEMORY GEMS.

From the lowest depth there is a path to the highest height.—Carlyle.

A man seldom loses the respect of others until he has lost his own.
—F. W. Robertson

There are certain things we feel to be beautiful and good, and we must hunger after them.—George Eliot

The man who thinks himself inferior to his fellows, deserves to be, and generally is.—William Black

It is characteristic of small men to avoid emergencies; of great men to meet them.—Charles Kingsley

Every man has characteristics which make him a distinct personality; a different individual from every other individual. It is an interesting fact that a man cannot change his nature, though he may conceal it; while no art or application will teach him to know himself, as he really is, or as others see him.

If the idea of humanity carry with it the corresponding idea of a physical, intellectual, and moral nature—if it be this trinity of being which constitutes the man,—then let us think of the first or the second elements as we may, it is the third which completes our conception. Let us praise the mechanism of the body to the utmost; let it be granted that the height and force of our intellect bespeaks a glorious intelligence; still our distinctive excellence and preeminence lies in moral and spiritual perfection.

There are those who think and speak as if manhood consisted in birth or titles, or in extent of power and authority. They are satisfied if they can only reckon among their ancestors some of the great and illustrious, or if noble blood but flow in their veins. But if they have no other glory than that of their ancestors; if all their greatness lies in a name; if their titles are their only virtues; if it be necessary to call up past ages to find something worthy of our homage,—then their birth rather disparages and dishonors them.

That these creatures lay claim to the name and the attributes of man, is a desecration. Man is a *noble* being. There may be rank, and title, and ancestry, and deeds of renown, where there is no intellectual power. Nor would we unduly exalt reason. There may be mental greatness in no common degree, and yet be a total absence of those higher moral elements which bring our manhood more clearly into view. It is the combination of intellectual power and moral excellence which goes to make the perfect man.

The world wants a man who is educated all over; whose nerves are brought to their acutest sensibility; whose brain is cultured, keen, and penetrating; whose hands are deft; whose eyes are alert, sensitive, microscopic; whose heart is tender, broad, magnanimous, true. Indeed, the only man who can satisfy the demands of an age like this, is the man who has been rounded into perfectness by being cultured along all the lines we have indicated in the foregoing pages.

This education must commence with the very first opening of the infant mind. Our lessons will multiply and be of a still higher character with the progress of our years. Truth may succeed truth, according to the mental power and capacity; nor must our instruction cease till the probationary state shall close. Our education can finish only with the termination of life.

Every one is conscious of a most peculiar feeling when he looks at anything whose formation or development is imperfect. Let him take up an imperfectly-formed crystal, or an imperfectly-developed flower, and he can scarcely describe his feelings. The same holds true as to the organization and structure of the human body. Who ever contemplates stunted growth, or any kind of visible deformity, with complacency and satisfaction? And why should we not look for full mental development, and for the most perfect moral maturity? If what is imperfect constitutes the exception in the physical world, why should it be otherwise in the world of mind and of morals? Is it a thing to be preferred, to be stunted, and little, and dwarfish, in our intellectual and moral stature? Or do we prefer a state of childhood to that of a perfect man? If the mind is the measure of the man, and if uprightness constitutes the noblest aspect of life, then our advancement in knowledge and in righteousness should appear unto all men.

There is a god in the meanest man; there is a philanthropist in the stingiest miser; there is a hero in the biggest coward,—which an emergency great enough will call out. The blighting greed of gain, the chilling usages and cold laws of trade, encase many a noble heart in crusts of selfishness; but great emergencies break open the prison doors, and the whole heart pours itself forth in deeds of charity and mercy.

The poor and unfortunate are our opportunity, our character-builders, the great schoolmasters of our moral and Christian growth. Every kind and noble deed performed for others, is transmuted into food which nourishes the motive promoting its performance, and strengthens the muscles of habit. Gladstone, in the midst of pressing duties, found time to visit a poor sick boy whom he had seen sweeping the street crossings. He endeared himself to the heart of the English people by this action more than by almost any other single event of his life; and this incident is more talked about to-day than almost any of his so-called greater deeds.

Not what men do, but what their lives promise and prophesy, gives hope to the race. To keep us from discouragement, Nature now and then sends us a Washington, a Lincoln, a Kossuth, a Gladstone, towering above his fellows, to show us she has not lost her ideal.

We call a man like Shakespeare a genius, not because he makes new discoveries, but because he shows us to ourselves,—shows us the great reserve in us, which, like the oil-fields, awaited a discoverer,—and because he says that which we had thought or felt, but could not express. Genius merely holds the glass up to nature. We can never see in the world what we do not first have in ourselves.

"Every man," says Theodore Parker, "has at times in his mind the ideal of what he should be, but is not. In all men that seek to improve, it is better than the actual character. No one is so satisfied with himself that he never wishes to be wiser, better, and more perfect."

The ideal is the continual image that is cast upon the brain; and these images are as various as the stars; and, like them, differ one from another in magnitude. It is the quality of the aspiration that determines the true success or failure of a life. A man may aspire to be the best billiard-player, the best coachman, the best wardroom politician, the best gambler, or the most cunning cheat. He may rise to be eminent in his calling; but, compared with other men, his greatest height will be below the level of the failure of him who chooses an honest profession. No jugglery of thought, no gorgeousness of trappings, can make the low high, the dishonest honest, the vile pure. As is a man's ideal or aspiration, so shall his life be.

But when all this has been said, it still remains true that much of the difference between man and man arises from the variety of occupations and practices,—a certain special training which develops thought and intelligence in special directions. All men meet, however, on the common level of common sense. A man's thought is indicated by his talk, by verbal expression. Mental action and expression is affected by the senses, passions, and appetites.

Whatever great thing in life a man does, he never would have done in that precise way except for the peculiar training and experience which developed him; and no single incident in his life, however trifling, may be excepted in the work of rounding him out to the exact character he becomes.

The poet is really calling for what we regard as the ideal man, when he says:

"God give us men. A time like this demands
Strong minds, great hearts, true faith and ready hands:
Men whom the lust of office does not kill;
 Men whom the spoils of office cannot buy;
Men who possess opinions and a will;
 Men who have honor—men who will not lie;
Men who can stand before a demagogue
 And scorn his treacherous flatteries without winking;
Tall men, sun-crowned, who live above the fog
 In public duty, and in private thinking."

XXXV.

WHAT CONSTITUTES GOOD CITIZENSHIP.
MEMORY GEMS.

A great nation is made only by worthy citizens.—Charles Dudley Warner

Nothing is politically right that is morally wrong.—O'Connor

The noblest principle in education is to teach how best to live for one's country.—G. T. Balch

The good citizen will never consent that his voice and vote shall sanction a public wrong.—A. M. Gow

Let our object be, our country, our whole country, and nothing but our country.—D. Webster

An old English picture represents a king, with the motto beneath, "I govern all;" a bishop, with this sentence, "I pray for all;" a soldier, with the inscription, "I fight for all;" and a farmer, who reluctantly draws forth his purse, and exclaims with rueful countenance, "I pay for all." The American citizen combines in himself the functions of these four. He is king, prophet, warrior, and laborer. He governs, prays, and fights for himself, and pays all expenses.

It is neither desirable nor possible, however, for men to be wholly independent of one another. Their very nature reveals the fact that they are intended to be associated in the bonds of mutual intercourse and affection; and such forms of associated life we see all about us, in the life of the family, the community, and the nation.

For a body of human beings to attempt to live together without regard for each other's interests, would be certain to lead to confusion, if not to disaster. There would be no security for life or property; no recognized standard of values; no ready and certain means of communication; nor any of the higher conveniences which mark the life of our own land and age. That which is needed to insure these necessary benefits, is some common understanding, or some such generally accepted agreement, as finds expression in those forms of government which have, for these very reasons, become common to all civilized lands.

It is in this idea of associated life that citizenship finds its real beginning. But between the formulation of the idea, and such citizenship as we now enjoy, there have been long centuries of slow growth and steady development. Each of these succeeding centuries has marked a decided improvement in the condition of mankind; and the outlook for the future of the race is more hopeful at the present than in any period of the past.

Men like to praise old times. They are fond of telling about "the good old days," when there was simplicity, and a rude but rugged virtue, and men were gay and happy. But if you were to take these men up, and carry them back there, and let them sleep where men slept then, and let them eat what men ate then, and let them do what men had to do then, and take from them what men did not have then,—you would hear the most piteous whining and complaining that ever afflicted your ears.

Do not be misled by such of our empty-headed reformers as would tell you that the workman's lot is harder at the present than in the far-away centuries of the past; for their statements cannot be verified, but are untruthful and pernicious in the highest degree. The sober, industrious, self-respecting artisan of to-day has the privilege of entrance to many places and families which were closed against the merchants and manufacturers of one hundred years ago; and he stands possessed of opportunities such as were not possible even to the men of the last generation.

Citizenship stands inseparably connected with the family. The family is practically a little state in itself, embodying on a smaller scale, all those vital and fundamental principles which make up the larger life of the nation. It is in the family that we first come under government. Our earliest lessons in obedience are those which arise from the authority of our parents and guardians. It is in the home that we discover that we cannot do altogether as we please, but that others, as well as ourselves, must be regarded. And it will not be difficult to discern that, in the various phases of home life, we have represented almost all the forms of government which have become embodied in the various kinds of national administration now prevailing in the various parts of the earth.

In a well-ordered home, the authority would be such that every one could have the largest freedom of action consistent with the general good. When the freedom of any one made itself a cause of annoyance to the rest, it would have to be curtailed. As fast as the children grew to deserve more liberty, it would be given them; but always on condition that they prove themselves worthy to be entrusted with this larger life.

But with this increase of freedom and privilege, comes the increase of responsibility. Every member of the family who is old enough to appreciate its privileges, is old enough to share its burdens. Some specific duties should be assigned to each, however simple these may be; and for the performance of these duties, each should be held to be personally responsible. Precisely this is needed in the larger sphere of the state; and when this can be attained and maintained, the good of the state will be both effectually and permanently assured.

A true lover of his country will have, as his ruling idea, that the state is for the people, and that America has been made to make and sustain happy Americans. No nation is in a satisfactory condition when large portions of its population are discontented and miserable. The comfortable classes will generally take care of themselves; but they need to know that their own prosperity is bound up with the condition of the uncomfortable classes. And even if it were not so, it would be their duty to advocate such social reforms as would tend to raise men intellectually, morally, and circumstantially. The carrying into effect of all this opens up a vast realm of service for the public good; and the proper performance of this service, in all its several branches, constitutes good citizenship.

Speaking in general terms, we may say that a citizen of a country is one born in that country. If you were born in the United States, then you are a citizen of the United States. This one simple fact endows you with all the privileges of our great nation, and, at the same time, lays upon you a measure of responsibility for the nation's welfare.

In addition to those who are trained for American citizenship in American homes, we have among us a large body of men who are "citizens by adoption." Millions of people have emigrated to America; and to these it has become the country of their own free choice.

We are sorry to observe, in certain quarters, a growing disposition to regard all immigrants as "a bad lot"; for while we concede that many of those who come here, might certainly be much better than they are, we would yet remind you that these "citizens by adoption" have repeatedly proved their loyalty to our national institutions, and their willingness to die in following our national flag.

Every good citizen will give attention to public affairs. He will not only vote for good men and good measures, but he will use his personal influence to have others do the same. Ours is a government of the people, and is neither better nor worse than the people make it. We should study the needs of our country, and keep ourselves well informed on all the current questions of the day, and then, by an honest and intelligent exercise of the privileges which the nation grants us, prove ourselves citizens of the very highest type.

XXXVI.

THE CITIZEN AND THE HOME.

MEMORY GEMS.

The hand that rocks the cradle rules the world.—Anon

The fireside is the seminary of the nation.—Goodrich

Early home associations have a potent influence upon the life of the State.—Child

Nothing proves more ruinous to the State than the defective education of the women.—Aristotle.

The sorest spot in our municipal and national condition, is the decadence of the home idea.—G. H. Parkhurst

The fact that children are so long in growing up, and pass so many years together under the care of their father and mother, is most important in the history of the race. During this long period of growth in the home they become fitted, as they could not in any other way, to take their places in the larger world of men and women. If children remained with their parents as short a time as the young of animals do, it is probable that men would never have risen above the state of barbarism. The home has been the great civilizer of the world.

The home is more than the family dwelling; it is the seat of the family life; and the family life stands to the life of the nation in the same relation as the index to the volume, or the expression of the countenance to the feeling of the heart. Our Saxon race has been distinguished from its historic beginnings for its love of personal liberty, and is the only race that has ever been able perfectly to realize this blessing in its highest and noblest form.

If the word home could be squeezed into the language of the savage, it could have no such meaning for him as it possesses for us. The hut of the savage is simply a place to eat in and sleep in. He selects no spot on which to plant, and build, and educate. He claims to occupy so much territory as will furnish him with subsistence, but his "home," if he really has one, is in the forest, like the game he hunts. It is a fact beyond dispute, that all migratory people are low down in the scale of civilized life.

The homes of any people are the very beginnings of its progress, the very centers of its law and order, and of its social and political prosperity. They are the central points around which the crystallizing and solidifying processes of national life and growth can alone be carried forward. We do not give sufficient prominence to this fact, in our estimate of the forces which build up our national life. We recognize art and science, agriculture and industry, politics and morality; but do we realize, as we should, that, beneath all these, as the great foundation rock upon which they all must rest, lies the home. Or, to change the figure, the homes of our people are the springs out of which flow our national life and character. They are the schools in which our people are trained for citizenship; for when a young man leaves the paternal roof, his grade and quality as a citizen is, as a rule, fully determined.

The training of a good citizen must begin at the cradle, and be continued through the plastic period of boyhood and carried forward by his parents, until the youth crosses his native threshold to act his part and assume his responsibilities in the broader field of his own independent life.

The home life of New England has been the most potent force, in the building of this great nation. The homes of our Puritan ancestors were really the birthplaces of these United States. What then was the character of these homes? They were simple and even rude, as considered externally—and especially when contrasted with the homes of the New Englanders of to-day. But within, there was love and loyalty, reverence and faith. In the early homes of New England there were so many strong fibers running from heart to heart, and knitting all together,—and so many solid virtues woven into the daily life,—that their influence has done much to make our nation what it is.

A young man trained in such a home, will usually become an example of sobriety, industry, honesty, and fidelity to principle. He will be felt to be part of the solid framework which girds society and helps to keep it healthy,—a kind of human bank, on which the community may draw to sustain its best interests, and to promote its noblest forms of life.

The home is the birthplace of true patriotism; and a true patriotism is one of the first and most important characteristics in the upbuilding of any nation. It is not the wild plebeian instinct that goes for our country right or wrong, which forms the real element of our strength. Love of country, to be a real help and safeguard, must be a sentiment great enough to be moral in its range and quality. Neither the power of numbers, nor mere oaths of allegiance, will suffice. Patriotism always falls back upon the home life and the home interests for its inspiration and its power.

Whatever crosses the threshold to desolate the hearth, touches to the quick one of the strongest sentiments of our nature. The old Latin battle cry, "For our altars and our firesides," is still the most potent word which can be given to our soldiers, as they advance upon the foe; and the man who will not go forward, even to the death, for these, is rightly counted as little better than a slave.

If you want a man upon whom you can rely in the hour of the nation's peril, select the man who loves his home; for in proportion as he loves his home, will he love his country which has protected it.

We therefore repeat that the homes of the people are the secret of our country's greatness. Acres do not make a nation great. Wealth cannot purchase grandeur and renown. Resources, however great and wonderful, cannot crown us with national honor and celebrity. The strength and prowess of any land lies in the character of its citizens; and their character depends largely upon the character of their homes.

XXXVII.

THE CITIZEN AND THE COMMUNITY.

MEMORY GEMS.

Municipal government should be entirely divorced from party politics.
—C. H. Parkhurst

Too many of our citizens fail to realize that local government is a worthy study.—John Fiske

Every citizen should be ready to do his full part in the service of the community in which he lives.—E. O. Mann

Each separate township needs men who will inspire respect and command confidence.—W. A. Mowry

Let the man who, without good excuse, fails to vote, be deprived of the right to vote.—W. H. H. Miller

Whenever men live in a community, they are placed under certain mutual obligations. Unless these obligations are carefully regarded the community life will be sure to prove a failure. Man is selfish as well as social. The weak must, therefore, be protected from the strong; and in this important work there are common interests which require united action. This united action may be for the common defense of the community, or for the general welfare of all.

The unit of government is generally the town, or as it is called in many parts of our country, the township. A town includes the people who are permanent residents within a certain limited and prescribed territory, usually occupying but a few square miles.

The government of a town, or township, is in the hands of the people permanently residing within the limits of that township. These people combine together for the protection and mutual good of all. This is the fundamental principle of government. To carry on this government and make the necessary provisions for the mutual good of the inhabitants of the town, taxation is resorted to. The people, therefore, come in contact with the government first of all at this point.

Taxes are levied by a majority vote of the citizens assembled in town meeting, such meetings being usually held once a year, in order that the moneys necessary to be raised, and the business to be done for the welfare of the people, may receive regular and careful attention.

Where the population is dense and houses are placed close together, so that within a small area there is a large body of inhabitants, thegovernment is generally under the form of a city.

Our republican government, which, after making all due allowances, seems to work remarkably well in rural districts, in the state, and in the nation, has certainly been far less successful as applied to cities. Accordingly our cities have come to furnish topics for reflection to which writers and orators fond of boasting the unapproachable excellence of American institutions do not like to allude.

Fifty years ago we were accustomed to speak of civil government in the United States as if it had dropped from heaven, or had been specially created by some kind of miracle upon American soil; and we were apt to think that in mere republican forms there was some kind of mystic virtue which made them a cure for all political evils. Our later experience with cities has rudely disturbed this too confident frame of mind. It has furnished facts which do not seem to fit our theory, so that now, our writers and speakers are inclined to regard our misgoverned cities with contempt.

It will best serve our purpose here, to outline the relation of the citizen to the township rather than to the city, because its management is less complex and, in most cases, is more complete and perfect.

Money is ordinarily raised by taxation for the following purposes, namely: the support of the public schools; making and repairing highways; the care of the poor; maintaining the fire department; paying the salaries of the town officers; paying for the detection and punishment of offenders against the law; maintaining burial grounds; planting shade trees; providing for disabled soldiers and sailors and their families; and, in general, for all other necessary expenses.

To carry on the work of a town, several officers are usually appointed. A town clerk keeps accurate records of all business transacted; records all births, marriages and deaths; makes the necessary returns to the county and the state, and serves as the agent of the town in its relation to the country at large. Officers usually known as selectmen or supervisors, attend to the general business of the town. The town treasurer receives and pays out all moneys raised for the carrying on of the town's affairs. A school committee, or board of education, is also needed to superintend all matters relating to our public schools. A surveyor of highways must be provided, in order that the streets and highways belonging to the town may be kept in proper condition; and an assessor and collector of taxes, to attend to the raising of supplies. A board of overseers of the poor is also needed, their duties being to provide for the support of paupers and the relief of the needy poor.

We do not profess to have fully covered the ground in this brief statement; but only to show that life, even in the smallest communities, must necessarily make heavy drafts upon the time and attention of a large number of individual citizens. But we desire to emphasize the fact, that each of these several offices furnishes opportunity for the employment either of a competent or an incompetent official, according to the care with which the selection is made. It therefore becomes the duty of every citizen to give personal attention to such matters, for if these places are filled by corrupt or even careless men, the interests of the community will be seriously imperiled, while if they are filled by honest and patriotic men, the success of the town and its affairs is practically assured.

Our one supreme object should be to raise the tone of our citizenship. The town or city will not become permanently better except as we who live in it become better. There are large sections in all our towns that yield to the guidance of corrupt and designing men for the reason that they are unreached by influences of a finer and more generous kind. Plans must be formulated by which we can come into touch with these lower quarters, and raise them quickly and surely to a higher level.

We all need to become better acquainted with the machinery of our local governments and with certain principles and statutes by which the motion of that machinery requires to be regulated. We cannot properly regulate the doings of our public servants except as we are familiar with the laws to which they are subject.

This question of obedience to law, can only be efficiently controlled by the continued watchfulness of the law-abiding portion of the community; and the situation in this respect is far more grave than most people imagine.

A recent writer speaking of the lack of a proper enforcement of the law says: "I was in a considerable Western city, with a population of seventy thousand, some years ago, when the leading newspaper of the place, commenting on one of the train robberies that had been frequent in the state, observed that so long as the brigands had confined themselves to robbing the railway companies and the express companies of property for whose loss the companies must answer, no one had greatly cared, seeing that these companies themselves robbed the public; but now that private citizens seemed in danger of losing their personal baggage and money, the prosperity of the city might be compromised, and something ought to be done,"—a sentiment delivered with all gravity, as the rest of the article showed.

This makes plausible the story of the Texas judge who is said to have allowed murderers to escape on points of law, till he found the value of real estate declining; then he carefully saw to it that the next few offenders were hanged.

We must not take too narrow a view of public life. All civilized governments consider themselves bound to perform other duties of an entirely different character from those which pertain to peace and justice. When our fathers framed the constitution of the United States, they gave in the preamble to that instrument an admirable definition of the province of government. This preamble reads as follows:

"We, the people of the United States, in order to form a more perfect union, establish justice, insure domestic tranquillity, provide for the common defense, promote the general welfare, and secure the blessings of liberty to ourselves and our posterity, do ordain and establish this constitution for the United States of America."

The motto of every good citizen should be, "the best means to promote the greatest good to the greatest number." The ends to be sought are the most healthy development, the highest and largest happiness to the whole people; for only in this manner can we accomplish our full duty.

XXXVIII.

THE CITIZEN AND THE NATION.

MEMORY GEMS.

Love your country and obey its laws.—Noah Porter

The sum of individual character makes national character.—E. C. Mann

The true defense of a nation lies in the moral qualities of its people.—Edwin C. Mason

Everything learned should be flavored with a genuine love of country.—E. Edwards

Noble ideas of citizenship and its duties strengthen the will of all patriots.—Merrill E. Gates

We are accustomed to say that our American government is "a government of the people, by the people, for the people." It is largely in this, its broad, comprehensive, and democratic character, that we so often venture to hold it up to view as a model which might be copied by the surrounding nations to their very great advantage. And certainly no thinking person will deny that we have much to be justly proud of in this respect; for our nation has neither parallel nor equal upon the face of the green earth.

But in a land like this, where the government is formed by its citizens, it can only be maintained by its citizens. Offices thus created must be filled, and the ship of state must be manned, and manned with a careful, honest, and patriotic crew, or it will be in danger of total wreck. In our times of peril we have been quick to see and to acknowledge this; and, more than once or twice, the nation has been saved by the prompt and patriotic action of the people. But it is not so easy a matter to keep our patriotism up to its noblest and its best when there is an absence of unusual or exciting causes to call it into play. We must therefore glance briefly at both these aspects of the case.

It is a requirement of long standing that, in case of war, every able-bodied citizen must go forth as a soldier, if the government shall so demand. He must, if really needful, help to save the state, even at the risk, or at the positive loss, of his own life. Such calls have been made by our government; and the manner in which our people have responded has been the glory of our nation and the wonder of the world.

The citizen must share the risks of his country, as well as its benefits. He must be willing to give protection to the rights and interests of his fellows, or he cannot rightly expect protection for his own. In this we are all so far agreed as to render anything like an argument entirely unnecessary; and we do not hesitate to brand all who fail us, under such circumstances, as unpatriotic and unworthy of the sympathy and esteem to which faithful citizenship entitles men.

Now look at the other aspect of the case. The public service is not only for times of war and tumult, but also for times of prosperity and peace; and the claims of the nation are no more to be slighted or shirked in the latter case than in the former. The ship of state must be manned, we say, and the public offices necessary to prosperity and progress must be filled. Many of these suffer unless filled by able and patriotic men; and the interests, for the preservation and forwarding of which these offices have been created, cannot be properly served.

The crying need of to-day is for men of public spirit; for men who will seek the highest welfare of their fellow-citizens in general; men of broad and generous views; men who look out upon life with an absence of that littleness and near-sightedness which cannot distinguish between public good and private interest.

Those men who will take no position in the service of their country, unless it is accompanied with a monetary compensation, are after all, very closely akin to the men who waited until bounties were offered before they would take service in connection with the Civil War; while, on the other hand, the men who are truly public-spirited, take pleasure in serving the public and are liberal beyond the requirement of the law.

It has been well said that "A public office is a sacred trust." Whoever engages in any duties of a public nature, is under the most solemn obligation to do those duties honestly and well. There are some public officials who, because they aid in the making of the laws, appear to think themselves higher than the law, and therefore at liberty to obey or to neglect its requirements, according as their personal inclinations shall direct. But this is not so; and it should be made clear to all such persons that they are in error.

The legislator is but a citizen, after all; and, as a citizen, he stands in precisely the same relation to the law as does his brother of the rank and file. Of all men, he should be obedient, and should labor to surround the law with every possible safeguard; for it is among the most precious and sacred of our earthly possessions. It is the charter of all true freedom. It is a power before whose awful majesty every man must bow, irrespective of outward position or personal influence. It must be reverenced, honored, and obeyed by all.

Now the facts show that there is a strange ignorance, or else a strange lack of conscience, in this matter, and that this is so wide-spread as to be almost universal. It seems to be a common opinion that there is no particular harm in cheating the government. If a politician secures a high government position, or a business man is fortunate enough to secure a large government contract, it seems to be expected that he will secure from these sources larger profits than would be possible anywhere else. In other words, it seems to be expected that the government will pay more for any service than can be obtained from an individual or from a private corporation, and that men will charge prices, and use deception and fraud when they work for the country, which if practiced upon private parties, would send them to prison and brand them with lifelong disgrace.

Respecting that purification and elevation of the ballot-box, for which so many of our thoughtful citizens are now pleading with more than usual earnestness, our own thought is that it can best be accomplished by the establishment and strict enforcement of an educational qualification for voters, and by a residence in the United States of at least ten years, before the voting privilege shall be bestowed. No man should be allowed to vote until he can read and write. No man should be allowed to put his hand upon the management of our public affairs until he can read and understand our Constitution in the language in which it is written.

One of the most ominous signs of the times is, that good men stand aloof from politics. They do this either because they do not fully appreciate the importance of their influence, or from the false conviction that their votes will do no good, or, in many other instances, because they consider their private business to be of more importance than the matters of the state. But, in point of fact, the uplifting of the moral tone of our country is a service of the most importance; and, even if we consider ourselves alone, it is still true that we cannot afford to pass it lightly by.

As citizens of the United States we stand possessed of a most wondrous heritage; and what the civil authorities require of us, within their own proper sphere, should be considered in the light of a binding duty. As Professor Dole has pointed out, "We have seen magnificent cities rising on the borders of the streams, and pleasant villages dotting the hills; a flourishing commerce whitens the ripples of the lakes; the laugh of happy children comes up to us from the cornfields; and as the glow of the evening sun tinges the distant plains, a radiant and kindling vision floats upon its beams, of myriads of men escaped from the tyrannies of the Old World and gathered here in worshiping circles to pour out their grateful hearts to God for a redeemed and teeming earth."

Surely all that is worth preserving. Surely we will not allow so rich a heritage to run waste. Surely we will support a nation whose past is bright with glorious achievements, and whose future glows with the light of a promise so radiantly beautiful. We need only remind you, therefore, that the truest and most useful citizens of our country are those who invigorate and elevate their nation by doing their duty truthfully and manfully; who live honest, sober, and upright lives, making the best of the opportunities for improvement that our land affords; who cherish the memory and example of the fathers of our country, and strive to make and keep it just what they intended it to be.

XXXIX.

THE IDEAL CITIZEN.

MEMORY GEMS.

Voters are the uncrowned kings who rule the nation.—Morgan

A second-rate man can never make a first-rate citizen.—J. S. White

Every good man in politics wields a power for good.—M. C. Peters

If you want a clean city, vote to place the government in clean hands.—Dr. Mc Glynn

The ideal citizen is the man who believes that all men are brothers, and that the nation is merely an extension of his family.—Habberton

We may now proceed to bring our studies to a close. All that has been said, from the beginning, has been gradually but surely focusing itself upon a single point; for the development of all these several faculties and powers leads directly to the forming of a well-rounded and fully-developed manhood.

A fully-developed manhood is the highest possible human achievement, and includes within itself all that can be desired; and for this higher manhood we now make our final and most urgent plea.

The real man is discovered in the sum total of his ideas; for it is in these that his life takes shape and character, it is in these that his true self comes into view. The real power of the true man lies in his being able to turn his thoughts inward upon himself; to so gauge and measure his own powers as to put them to the best uses; and to stand aloof from those positions and practices for which he finds himself to be unfitted.

The simple application of this rule to the practical affairs of to-day, would diminish the number of our machine politicians by about four fifths. We are loaded down, almost to the breaking point, with politicians who do not understand politics, and who advocate measures which are not for the public good, because the public good is not the end for which they strive. But the fault is in the men themselves, rather than in our political system. They must first be made manly, before they can be made truly useful. They must first learn to govern themselves, before they can successfully carry forward the work of governing the nation. They must be taught that bluster is not argument, and that to go through the motions of political service does not in the least aid in the promotion of the public welfare. A single service rendered from the heart is often of more value than a whole life of noisy and showy pretense; but again we say that such service is almost always the result of a thoughtful and considerate manliness.

All this applies with equal force to the private citizen. A sturdy but quiet independence; a genuine love of righteousness and truth; a life of uprightness and integrity, of honesty and fair dealing; an absence of cringing and paltering, and of that miserable and contemptible fawning upon the rich, and that silly and despicable worship of those in place and power, which is too frequently to be observed;—all these things, and others, must receive care and attention before the ideal stage of manhood can be reached.

The manly man is a thinking being. By this we do not mean to say that he imagines that he is running the universe, and that no one but himself is acquainted with the secrets of its mechanism; but that he has a right to weigh all questions in the scales of his own reason, and to draw his own conclusions from the facts presented to his mind. If he be truly a man, he will hold to that which he feels to be true against all opposition, but will, with equal readiness, yield in all points where he discovers himself to be in the wrong. Instead of going through life in political leading-strings, bending to the will of one man, and gulping down the opinions of another, he will stand upon his own feet, put his own vertebral column to its legitimate use of sustaining his body, and his own mind to its legitimate use of directing the issues of his life.

The ideal citizen will also be a gentleman. By this term, we do not mean the milk-and-water, kid-gloved creature, who so often attempts to pass muster in this connection. All that we have asked for in the man, we insist on in the gentleman. Sturdy independence, vigorous thought, mental and moral uprightness, and a backbone as strong as a bar of steel,—but all tempered with a gentleness of disposition and a courtesy of manner which brings every natural faculty and power beneath its sway, and yet leaves principle and righteousness entirely undisturbed.

The real gentleman is, above all else, courteous and considerate. He is master of himself, and that at all points,—in his carriage, his temper, his aims, and his desires. Calm, quiet, and temperate, he will not allow himself to be hasty in judgment, or exorbitant in ambition; nor will he suffer himself to be overbearing or grasping, arrogant or oppressive.

The ideal citizen will also be, in the better sense of the word, a politician. Be careful to note here that we say, a politician *in the better sense*. We would have you distinguish, with the utmost clearness, between a politician and a partisan. The true politician, looking ever to the highest interests of the state, is a public benefactor; while it very frequently happens that the mere political partisan is a public nuisance, if not a public disgrace.

The man who sinks his country's interests in his own, and the man who sacrifices his personal advantages for the sake of his country's good, stand at the very opposite poles of human society. The man who swears by party watchwords, and moves amid the burning animosities of party strife, is centering his life in interests which may vanish like an evening cloud. Not in the loud clamors of partisan struggle, are we to find the secret highways which lead to national prosperity and progress, but in that quiet, thoughtful, careful study of the interests and events in which the national life is taking shape and color, and in the application to these of the great principles of righteousness and common sense.

This is about equal to saying that the ideal citizen will be a patriot. We have so mixed in our minds the two distinct ideas of patriotism and heroism, that we have need to pause for a moment, that we may disentangle ourselves from the meshes of this net of misconception, before we venture to proceed.

If we call for an illustration of patriotism, you point us to some Horatius or Leonidas of the olden times; or to some William Tell, or Ulysses Grant, of these more modern days. We do not say that these men were not patriots, and patriots of a high order too. But their circumstances were exceptional, and under these exceptional circumstances their patriotism made them heroes. But if you will enter into a careful study of the matter, you will find that it is the heroism, quite as much as the patriotism of their lives, which takes so strong a hold upon your hearts.

We therefore desire to place by the side of our beloved Grant, the man who, in the midst of a bitter struggle for bread, can barely manage by the closest possible economy to keep his family from want and shame, but who still sacrifices an hour's wages that he may go to the polls and vote the expression of his will, and thus support the measures which he honestly believes to be for the public good; and we desire to say that, on the ground of a true patriotism, we consider that the one is fully the equal of the other, and that there is a sense in which the man of smaller opportunities is the greater hero of the two.

There may be a thousand definitions of heroism, but the patriot is simply "a man who places his country's interests before his own." He is a patriot who fills well his station in life whether public or private, who loves peace and promotes order, who labors to uphold the good and to put down the bad. He is a patriot who uses all his advantages of friendship, acquaintance, business connection, social position and the like, in such a manner as to make these helps and not hindrances to his country's progress. He is a patriot who seeks to aid in all movements that look to the instruction, elevation, and permanent betterment of his fellow-citizens, and to put down all such movements or institutions as tend to demoralize and degrade them. Such is the patriotism we plead for; and such patriotism and ideal citizenship are, in our minds, just one and the same thing.

Milton Keynes UK
Ingram Content Group UK Ltd.
UKHW040839141024
449705UK00006B/364